A Savvy Approach to Book Sales

Marketing Advice to Get the Buzz Going

A Savvy Approach To Book Sales

Elaine Wright Colvin

PUBLISHING

Belleville, Ontario, Canada

A Savvy Approach to Book Sales
Copyright © 2000 Elaine Wright Colvin

This book contains information gathered from many sources. It is published for general reference and not as a substitute for independent verification by users when circumstances warrant. It is sold with the understanding that neither the author nor publisher is engaged in rendering any legal advice. The publisher and author disclaim any personal liability, either directly or indirectly, for advice or information presented within. Although the author and publisher have used care and diligence in the preparation, and made every effort to ensure the accuracy and completeness of information contained in this book, we assume no responsibility for errors, inaccuracies, omissions, or any inconsistency herein. Any slights of people, places, publishers, books or organizations are unintentional.

ISBN: 1-55306-105-5
Illustrations by Sylvia Draaistra

Essence Publishing is a Christian Book Publisher dedicated to furthering the work of Christ through the written word. For more information, contact: 44 Moira Street West, Belleville, Ontario, Canada K8P 1S3.
Phone: 1-800-238-6376. Fax: (613) 962-3055.
E-mail: info@essencegroup.com
Internet: www.essencegroup.com

Printed in Canada
by

Essence
P U B L I S H I N G

Table of Contents

Network with Key Players
Keep God in the Equation

Develop a Marketing Theme
Think About Writing Another Book
Create a Newsletter
Use Business Cards
Develop Useful Specialty Products
Develop Key Contacts with the Influencers
Partner with Other Author/Speakers
Stay Involved with Events That Make the News

What About Classified Ads?
Book Reading List
Periodical List
Publicists You May Want to Contact and/or Hire

The Christian Bookstore Industry in Canada
Publicity and Book Reviews
Other Sources of Information

Acknowledgments

This book is the result of many helping hands. A debt of gratitude and thanks to:

The staff at Essence who back their authors 100 percent and desire to see each one succeed in spreading the Good News through the printed word, and who want to help writers get their story out to the waiting readers.

My good friends, Gus and Beryl Henne, for their friendship and encouragement, their marketing creativity and vision to help authors tell their story, and their quest for accuracy in their fact-checking and proofreading skills.

My husband, Bob, for his continuous technical support in conquering my computer problems, and his unending faith in me to write yet another book under tight deadline.

My self-published author friends who paved the way by giving me great stories to share about their books and their successes.

Introduction

Welcome to the world of being a published author. Now that you have decided to be a home-based entrepreneur, the fun—and work—really begins. You are now self-employed, running a business, and becoming a public relations firm all at once. You control your own schedule, have all the responsibility in how much money you make, and can run your business the way you want to (except for what you have to report to local, state, and federal agencies). But you're not alone—some estimates say that as much as 20 percent of our workforce is now self-employed. And the number of people working at home is climbing steadily, too.

With all of our modern conveniences: computers, faxes, modems, e-mail, answering machines, pagers, photocopy machines, and online services, it has become incredibly convenient to run a business from your home.

Since you have taken or are about to take the big leap of faith of becoming an author, it's time to get serious about book promotion, author promotion, and selling your product.

And, like it or not, you're going to have to accept the fact that you're in the sales business. You have invested a sizable amount of time and money to get to this point—so, there's no turning back now. Successful salespeople tell you that your attitude is as important as what you're selling and to whom.

> *You must make it happen.*
> *You must speak, sell, promote, push, hype, badger,*
> *preach, teach—whatever it takes to get others to believe*
> *in you and your message.*

As a self-publisher, one of your first challenges has been to pinpoint your niche market for this book. Because you know the market for your book, you know who the likely candidates are to buy your book, and you can carefully target your promotion efforts. Against that grid, you'll be able to select the media methods which will enable you to reach your audience. Targeting your book's message to the proper audience is probably the most challenging part of your job. Of course, your best starting point is always your own ministry platform.

Dan Poynter, author of *The Self-Publishing Manual,* says, "Small publishers are like a boutique with a narrow line for a highly-targeted market (which is easier to reach)." Remember, you are just one among the many hungry authors. At this particular time in the United States and Canada, there are hundreds of thousands of self-publishers. In 1999, there were a reported 150,772 books published in the United States, with self-published books being the fastest growing segment of the publishing industry.

Says Steve Meyer, the self-publisher of six books: "The publishing business has always been very competitive, and it is that much more so now with the glut of self-publishers inundating book markets. It seems that books are every-where and everyone has one out." Even though you are not guaranteed a large amount of return on your investment, there are numerous things you can to do ensure that it will not all have been in vain. When you know your market and use all the avenues available to you to promote to that mar-ket, your result will be successful book sales.

Determine how big a splash you want to make—need to make—in order to give your book the proper send-off and attract the greatest audience attention. You must make it happen. You must speak, sell, promote, push, hype, badger, preach, teach—whatever it takes to get others to believe in you and your message. After all, if you didn't believe in it, you wouldn't have plunked down $1,200-$20,000 (the average is $12,000) to have your book published. And you wouldn't have given a year or more of your life to writing it. If you don't do the promotion, who will?

If you are not out there trying to make your book stand out, you will simply be lost in the crowd of new books that roll off the presses each year. You are the one who can tout the ben-efits and create eager waiting readers. This is your baby and no one cares as much about its message as you do. If you are hes-itating at this point, if you really can't see yourself as a speaker and promoter, if you don't want to be actively involved in the marketing process, then writing and publishing a book is not for you. There is no way for any author not to be actively involved in promotion and selling. Simply placing advertise-ments in magazines does not sell books—well maybe one or two but certainly not enough to pay the printer or to sell many books. If you do not pick up the challenge of getting the news out about your new book and reaching your potential cus-tomers, you'll end up with a garage full of books.

At this stage in the game, you may not be quite sure of yourself. If you're feeling slightly timid and overwhelmed, get help! Begin by reading—we assume that's why you're starting with this book. After you know what you need to do, determine if you can do it or if you will have to hire the help of others more capable than yourself. But most of all, set your plan of action in motion.

It pays to remember that you did not go into publishing to get rich. If that was your end goal, your odds of success would probably be better if you took up playing the lottery. Your biggest challenge in becoming a self-publisher is distribution—that is the hard part. If you're not willing to market your book anywhere and everywhere, to friends and strangers alike, to "cold call" on stores and people you don't know, and to risk rejection, then self-publishing is probably not for you. Unless you are independently wealthy and can hire people to perform all of the services that you are going to be needing, you must do the work of marketing.

A successful book takes an extraordinary amount of effort on the part of everyone involved. You must learn to use every avenue at your disposal—press releases, review copies, radio and TV appearances, autograph parties, lectures, seminars, promotional tie-ins, contacts with wholesalers and distributors, and more. And because you are your biggest asset, we are here to help you reach your fullest potential. Because you've invested countless hours and money to communicate with your audience, you probably know more about your book subject than most anyone. And it is by using your imagination, personality, initiative, and perseverance that you will be able to carry on a unique marketing plan to get your books to their waiting readers. All of these mentioned opportunities are free publicity that have been used in launching books. The key is to capitalize on all the available free publicity and keep the media coming back for more. Keep creating newsworthy events. But be realistic in your expectations. All publicity can be a help, but don't expect any single event or mention to make you an overnight success.

Richard Paul Evans, self-publisher of the famed *The Christmas Box*, says, "Self-publishing is like running in the Olympics without a country. They make you run outside the stadium. It's different from having a publisher because your focus [then] is on the reader, not the selling" (*Writer's Digest*, October 1999).

Marketing your book, whether self-published or not, is much like driving a car—as soon as you let your foot off the pedal, you lose momentum, sales drop, and you risk coming to a stand-still. As a published author, it is your responsibility to be persistent in marketing and finding ways to keep your book alive. When you persist long enough, your prime marketing tool—word-of-mouth—has the opportunity to get the buzz going.

ONE

Where to Start

Developing a market for any book requires an enormous amount of learning, if you want to do it right and be successful. Of course, it helps if you have published a book that has a huge waiting audience. But what can you do to get it into the marketplace? Like one successful author said, "It's not enough to know that there's a potential audience of a million readers out there. You must find them and sell to them. That's why most successful self-publishers first zeroed in on topics with localized or highly select audiences" (Franklynn Peterson and Judi Kesselman-Turkel in *The Author's Handbook*, p. 207). Hopefully, some of it you have already done, like checking on the competition before you decided to publish your book, and determining how large the market is for your book. So what next?

You are taking the plunge to become a business professional. It is therefore important that you understand being a professional is much more than just a look or an appearance—it is also an attitude. It's a "can do" attitude. It's an attitude that says, "I realize it may be tough going for a while, but I'm in it for the long haul and I will succeed."

Learn All You Can About Marketing

Developing a market is perhaps the most important step. Noting trends, your reading public, your target audience, specific channels for selling, and that all-important timing factor, determine what the odds are for your book to do really well in the marketplace. Do you know how to reach the appropriate people to promote this book and you as author? As marketing manager for your book and your company, it will be your job alone (unless you hire a publicist) to make the world aware of your book. This job starts before your book goes into production and continues through the life of the book. Newspapers, magazines, radio, TV, the speaking circuit—all play a part in the successful launch of any book.

A key to selling your work is *never stop learning*. As technology develops, and mergers, conglomerations, buyouts, and the Internet change the way people think and shop, it's more important than ever to keep a broad perspective on your profession.

See the bibliography in Chapter 10 of this book for ideas on where to start. Book publishing is a *big* industry and there's lots to know if you are going to survive. Knowing that the majority of books published sell fewer than 5,000 copies, and many sell fewer than 1,000 copies, may help you think realistically about your book.

It is fair to say that being a good salesperson is more important than being a good writer. Even work of poor quality can be sold to someone if the presentation is convincing enough, but the best work may go nowhere at all if not backed by an aggressive sales approach. For novice self-publishers, at least one thing is certain—it takes more time and effort to make a few sales than it did to do the actual writing.

Before Going to Press

- Pay Careful Attention to the Look of Your Book

There's no doubt about it—a book's cover has the power to make or break a sale. Often quoted is: "Your book title has three to five seconds to grab the attention of the casual browser." According to John Peterson, an independent designer with Koechel/Peterson & Associates Inc., a firm that creates covers for about a dozen CBA publishers, "Many books sell well even though they aren't really good books simply because they're well-designed, well-packaged, and seem to get the exposure that others don't."

David Visser, Managing Editor of Essence Publishing, stresses the importance of a well-designed cover. "We are constantly telling our writers that cover design is one of the most important elements of book production. Most successful books have well-designed covers." Because most books have small marketing budgets, the cover may be a consumer's first introduction to a book—and the goal is for it to make a favorable first impression. "Cover design becomes even more important when the author is unknown. Unless the author is somebody with instant recognition, the cover is the only thing that prompts a person to pick up a book," says Matthew Wall of Gospel Supplies in Tucson, Arizona.

Other cover trends noted as emerging in 2000 include: titles are getting smaller on covers; bright colors are common; special effects such as raised lettering and embossing are helping sales; designers are paying more attention to the back cover; the front cover draws attention to the book. Then most people flip to the back cover for more information—you have about thirty seconds to tell why this will be an intriguing book and thus hook the reader. The back cover includes details such as the benefits of reading the book, endorsements, and some details about the author.

A book is more likely to be purchased when it has an eye-catching front cover that gets the customer to pick it up, and an informative back cover that stresses benefits and convinces the reader there is something in it for him.

• Get the Big Name Endorsements

Getting well-known, credentialed people to review and endorse your book before it goes to press is essential. At the very least, two endorsements (also known as blurbs) are needed. Make a list of celebrities or key players in your book's field of interest who might give your book enthusiastic praise. Testimonials, recommendations, and/or endorsements all play a part in your credibility and giving your book the high-profile "send-off" it needs.

When soliciting endorsements before the book has been set in type, you may send out bound copies of your edited manuscript. Be sure to send a cover letter with an explanation and a SASE to aid in a speedy reply. Your major endorsements need to arrive before the cover copy goes to press. Late endorsements and testimonials may be used later in promotional materials. It's not enough to get the endorsements, it's even more important to determine how to use

LINDA HOSTELLEY

Essence author, Linda Hostelley, passed out many copies of her stories and poems long before she ever went to press. Her generous sharing paid off. The front of her book, *Touched by His Staff... Glimpses of How the Good Shepherd Touched My Life* (Essence, 1999), is filled with six pages of valuable testimonials from such influential people as: Bishop Earl Paulk, Cathedral of the Holy Spirit at Chapel Hill, Decatur, Georgia; Florence Littauer, Speaker and Founder of CLASS; Daniel L. Black, Editor of Pathway Press; Dan Elliott, Editor of Tyndale Publishers; and Rev. David A. Rice, Assistant to Dr. James Kennedy, Coral Ridge Ministries. By the time her book came off the press, she had several waiting audiences.

Linda wrote the WIN office, "Again I can't thank you enough for all your help in making this book a dream come true. Everyday I am receiving the most amazing comments about it. On February 13, I am going to be interviewed on a radio program for a half hour, and this Sunday, I have my first public book signing at my church of 800, and the following week, another one at our business. I have sold over 120 without doing any advertising and now have about 600 flyers going out to my following over the years. I just love my book and all that it will do to bring many into the kingdom." [Cost of book: $11.95, plus $2.55 shipping = total $14.50us. It will take seven to ten days to arrive. Send check or money order to: Linda Hostelley, PO Box 1763, Millsboro DE 19966. (302) 934-9558.]

them for maximum effectiveness. Endorsements may be used on book jackets and on advertising brochures. It's always a good idea to obtain permission before you use an endorsement. Testimonials and favorable comments from any letters you receive may be used creatively in future media packets and advertising brochures.

• Let a Distributor Review Your Book

If you are planning on using a distributor for your work, it is a good idea to have them review the book before you go to press. Since their main interest is in selling your work, they will be a good judge of your book's content and ability to stand up to the competition. Suggestions received before your book is actually printed can save you costly errors. Some distributors insist on quality controlling your product before they will promise you they can handle your book. Distributors may ask you to submit sketches of the front cover design, front and back cover copy, and a copy of the complete manuscript (prior to copyediting) in order to make reasonable suggestions for changes. Often they can make suggestions that will increase your book's marketability (including printing the name and address of your distributor in the book so additional orders can be generated). Submitting your work-in-progress during the early stages eliminates the risk of not having your book picked up by a distributor because they feel it is of inferior quality. A distributor who is right for your target audience will have a better grasp than most people on what it will take to make your book sell well.

When you have signed a deal with a distributor, you will want to make sure that your book cover graphics are supplied to them in time to make their catalog production.

When a book is introduced in a distributor's frontlist, the book cover becomes your most important marketing tool.

Have a Marketing Plan

Good marketing and strong promotion will pave the way for great sales. It takes a lot of energy and a strong belief in your product in order to be constantly promoting your book. Because the marketplace is so overcrowded with books, yours must have a distinct focus to stand out. Books are more specialized. Make sure you have an identifiable narrow focus that a sizable audience will identify with.

Marketing is a process. It is ever evolving and always changing. Keep records of where your sales come from, who tells who, and where you find the hot markets. Eventually you will have a way of determining what has worked best for you and cost the least in terms of effort and expense. On the other hand, you will know which avenues led to no sales at all. This will help you more carefully target your efforts in the future. But don't give up. Marketing takes time—a lot of time—and it may mean many months before you are really able to create the buzz you hope for.

Every now and then we hear a writer say, "Well, I'll just buy ads in several well-known Christian magazines." Great. That may help down the line in name recognition, but it rarely sells more than a handful of books. How many times have you bought a book from an unknown author because you saw it advertised in the classified ads of *Christianity Today* or *World* or *Charisma* magazine? Did I prove my point? Magazine and newspaper advertising can be a very expensive venture with little return on your dollar.

It is a commonly held truth that nonfiction benefits from publicity better than fiction. In most publishers' experience, nonfiction has a greater potential for breaking out or creating a buzz even many months after it is released. With the right book, the right author, and strong promotional efforts, anything can happen.

Explore other avenues of publicity (book reviews, fliers, brochures, postcards, the list could go on) before you plunk down your money in magazine and newspaper advertising.

Be aware that in order to sell lots of books you will also probably give a lot of books away. Make sure you allow for these giveaways in your profit/cost equation. Who gets the freebies? Anyone you are seeking a book review from; anyone you're hoping will want to interview you on radio, television, or in the newspaper; distributors, stores, anyone you're hoping will want to include your book in their product line; and then, of course, your long list of: family friends, associates, and others who helped you with the book or gave endorsements. Some sources believe that you should plan to give away at least 10 percent of your books. Another caution: Those give-away books normally come early in the game, so it may be several months before you start seeing any sales that will start to recoup your costs.

MARKETING PLAN FORMULA

- *Allow 10% of your books as give-aways*
- *Pre-sell 20-30% of your books*
- *Sell 20-30% at the book launch*

This accounts for 50% of your books. If your books have been priced right, the 40% that have been purchased will pay for 100% of the books you have ordered. The balance is sold over time as word-of-mouth picks up, as you develop and work with your audience, and as the give-aways reap their harvest.

Consult with the Experts

Authors who have already self-published their book are a good source of information for you. Contact companies like Essence who help authors publish their books. Write letters, make phone calls, talk to other authors at Writers Conferences. None of us will live long enough to have time to reinvent the wheel. It is wise to glean off the experiences of others. Writers love to talk about both their book and their publishing experiences. Take other self-published authors to lunch and pick their brains about marketing techniques that have worked well or fizzled. In publishing circles, you'll find that key players are always willing to share their experiences, knowledge, and resources.

Make inquiry of professional publicists and determine if they could better handle your publicity efforts—especially getting you the bookings on radio and television. For some, it's their full-time job and specialty, so they have the system down pat.

What features of your book do early reviewers particularly like? How can you make these into key selling features? If you are not confident in your ability to be the best judge of your book and how to sell it, gather a group of friends/ writers together for a brainstorming focus group. Good ideas bring about more ideas; personal referrals and contacts make good places to start.

Gather Necessary Resources

While your book is in production is an excellent time to do the groundwork for the launch of your long-awaited product. Your goal is to create a demand—a waiting audience—for your book. If they've never heard of it, they can't/

won't buy it, no matter how many bookstores you get it in or how successful you've been at securing a distributor.

This is the perfect time to submit excerpts from the book to the appropriate publications that you have already targeted as your reading audience. To help create the buzz for your book, excerpts should begin appearing about sixty days before publication and continue as long as you can find possible markets for interesting topics from your book. Because of the up-to-three month lead time at most publications, you must start lining up excerpt possibilities well in advance of your publication date.

Your query letter can take the form of your book's title and a short 150 to 200-word synopsis. Some publications will offer you an advertisement or a resource book announcement in lieu of payment for your article. That's not a bad deal. Try to get them both to run in consecutive issues. Always make sure the complete title and postpaid price of your book is included, as well as author, publisher, address, and telephone number. And don't forget to publicize the pre-publication discount price. Everyone loves a bargain.

Writing Magazine Articles

Select the chapters or sections of your book that can be adapted and rewritten as articles. This becomes an excellent way to expose your book to thousands of readers. Generally, such articles end with a footnote stating that the piece is from such and such a book, and list the title, author, publisher, and price. Sometimes other material from your book is suitable to use as a sidebar. The more magazine articles you get published, the more free publicity you are getting, and in the process you may be earning a good amount of extra money for the book excerpts.

Have a Good File System in Place

Be sure that you have a good information file system in place. This is largely a matter of expediency and individual taste: computer program, file folders, binders, 3" x 5" card file. Use anything that works for you—so you can put your hands on a needed piece of information in sixty seconds or less.

Try to get as many PR samples as you can from other authors or publicists. Send for writers guidelines from the periodicals you want to review your book. Obtain book review editors' names and addresses. Then get to work at writing: your press release, media kit, galley copy, cover letter, brochure, flier, ad postcard, bookmark, and database of potential customers—friends, associates, relatives, clubs.

If your book is appropriate for the CBA market, you may want to purchase from CBA the names and addresses of all the Christian member bookstores. This could be important even if you don't plan a massive mailing announcement, but rather might be taking driving tours of many states to get your books into the bookstores. A similar membership directory is available from NRB of the religious radio stations around the country. And there are sources for finding the home school magazines, as well as homeschool book and supply stores which are springing up in numerous locations.

In the meantime, where are you going to store all of those books once they are delivered from the printer? Don't make the mistake of putting them in a damp basement or garage. Long-term book warehousing demands a safe, dry environment. One author figured out that if your book is approximately 6" x 9" in size, and you order 5,000 copies, packed efficiently in boxes stacked six feet high, you'll need about thirty-six square feet of floor space. Pace it off—where can you put all those boxes?

Set goals and establish your priorities. There are logical steps that must be taken before you can go on to the next "thing" to get your marketing process in order (i.e. you have to have your printing done and copies made before you can start assembling media kits). Get a business plan outlined so you know where you're headed and how long it will take you.

FILES TO DEVELOP

- Advertising and Public Relations
- Articles
- Author and Speaker Contacts
- Book Reviews
- Bookstores/Contact Names
- Cover Letter Samples
- Canceled Checks
- Expenses/Tax Receipts
- Fairs, Festivals
- Galleys/Pre-Pub Samplers
- Invoices/Collections
- Letters to Editors
- Media Contacts
- Media Kits
- Networking Associations
- Newsletter Samples
- Phone Orders
- Photographs
- Press Releases
- Price Quotes from Vendors
- Radio Stations/Talk Show Hosts
- Speaking and Teaching Opportunities
- Tax Records
- Tracking Record of Books on Consignment
- Trade Shows, Conferences, Writers' Conferences

HOW TO ESTABLISH A REALISTIC SELLING PRICE FOR YOUR BOOK

1. Start with the production cost of your book to establish a cost per book.

2. Ideally, the retail price of a book should be between three and six times the production cost of the book. Multiply the cost per book by three, four, five and six. This gives you the selling range.

3. The type of book—fiction, nonfiction, poetry, family history. etc.—the number of pages, the content, and the kinds of similar books on the market will help determine whether the selling price should be at the higher range.

4. Then adjust this figure to reflect pricing habits in your community, i.e. $11.95 or $11.00 or $11.99.

SETTING UP MY BUSINESS

How much money do I need to invest in my
        promotional materials?
Where will this money come from?
How many hours a day can I devote to marketing?
How many days a week?
Will I need to hire outside help...
        for publicity? for delivering books?
        for baby-sitting? for housecleaning?
        for storage of books? for shipping and handling?
        for doing direct mail blitzes?

What books do I need to invest in?

Do I have a good bookkeeping/tax system in place?

Do I need a business license in my city? state?

Do I have good office procedures in place...

> for handling orders?
> for filing PR material?
> for creating a mailing list?
> for taking phone orders?

Do I know where to secure the best services for...

> graphic designer/desktop publishing?
> artist/illustrator?
> photographer?
> web site provider?
> printing, duplicating? addressing, mailing?
> mailing lists?

Do I have all the necessary equipment or will I need to purchase...

> desk and desk chair, files, shelving?
> telephones, cellular phone, pager?
> fax machine, phone-fax-modem manager?
> answering machine, copier, calculator?
> postage meter and scale?

BREAK EVEN POINT

Divide the production cost of your book by the retail price of your book. This number is equal to your break even point. Once you have sold this many books, you have recovered your direct production costs.

TWO

When to Begin Promotion

One best-selling self-published author says, "Even before your book is published you should be marketing it." Dr. Jeffrey Lant says, "If you're talking on the subject of your book—and if not, why not—you will thus have the opportunity to promote it at least a month before your talk, at your talk, and through either a review of your talk and/or a review of your book, after your talk" (quoted in *For All the Write Reasons,* compiled by Patricia C. Gallagher, p. 202-203).

Pre-Publication Announcements

It is tempting to want a four-color glossy flier to introduce your book to your waiting fans. But printing thousands of fliers in the quality and quantity you need can get very expensive. This is a good time to find a photographer and/or graphic artist to use as your consultant. If you acquired a good mailing list and your fans are waiting, the money and effort to do early announcements can bring in a huge stack of pre-publication orders and money. Make sure your fliers request pre-payment. And no matter how good of a writer you are, always run your final copy past a proof-reader or copy editor. Typos and small errors can be costly.

Promotional opportunities are all around you. This is not the time to be shy. Send your pre-publication announcement to all the clubs and professional associations you belong to, to book trade publications and reviewers, and to anyone else you have on your waiting list who doesn't need to see your book in order to start promoting it. Don't forget college and university alumni letters, company in-house newsletters, family reunion publications, and other club and house organs. Most of these groups publish magazines or newsletters with a special "News of Members" column, so it's a perfect place to begin your publicity efforts. But don't just announce your book—Sell It!

Of course, to make such pre-publication announcements work, you must know the ultimate retail price of your book, the discount price you will offer on pre-publication orders, and the cut-off date for those discounted orders.

Professional business practice demands that for all of those pre-publication orders you receive, you fill them (mail the book) within the 30-day grace period of your announced publication date. Announced publication dates should never be more than four months away. Mark Ortman, author of *A Simple Guide to Self-Publishing* (Wise Owl Books), advises: "Set a publication date far enough in the future to give you time to print, submit for review, announce your book and generate advance sales. Your publication date is not the date

SOON TO BE RELEASED

Essence Publishing announces the April publication of *A Savvy Approach to Selling Books ... Marketing Advice to Get the Buzz Going,* by Elaine Wright Colvin. A Must Read For Anyone Self-Publishing or Being Published by a Small to Medium Size Press. You, the author, must make it happen. You must speak, sell, promote, push, hype, badger, preach, teach—whatever it takes to get others to believe in you, your message, and purchase your book. *Special pre-publication price:* $8.95US/ $11.95CDN until April 15th (add $2 postage). After April 15th: $9.95US/$12.95CDN. Order from our WIN OFFICE, PO Box 11337, Bainbridge Island WA 98110 (206) 842-9103; or Essence Publishing, 44 Moira St. W., Belleville, Ontario, Canada K8P 1S3. 1-800-238-6376; www.essencegroup.com.

your book comes back from the printer. The publication date is when you are releasing your book for sale to the public. The best publication date for the self-publisher is the first quarter of the year because this allows your copyright date to live a full year and still be new."

Many authors have found that it pays to ship in the Priority mail envelopes and boxes available FREE at US post offices. Why pay for mailers when there are many shipping supplies available from the post office?

If you cannot ship the books within the allotted time, you must alert the buyer that there is a delay in shipping.

This buys you another 30-day grace period. However, if you still cannot ship the books to fulfill the orders that you have in hand, then you must refund all money received to date. Therefore, be very careful and work with your publisher or printer to announce the correct delivery date of your book.

Book Fliers and Brochures

A flier or brochure should be designed as soon as you know all of the pertinent details about your book: title, picture of book jacket, content, author bio, size of book, number of pages, illustrations, type of binding, ISBN and Library of Congress numbers, ordering information, and price. Keep it simple, yet be sure that it has a hook that will grab the attention of your intended audience.

Hooks that demand attention are those that address needs. The six basic needs are: to feel better, look better, earn money, save money, save time, and conquer specific fears. Your introductory statement should immediately communicate your book's ability to meet at least one of these basic needs or to offer solutions to frustrations and problems. If you can position your book as addressing any of these needs, you can get consumers to buy your book. Remember, whether you are writing or speaking, you only have a few seconds to grab someone's attention. Use your most powerful words to motivate and persuade your book buyers.

Fliers may be one side $8\,1/2$" x 11", two-sided, or even take the style of a two-fold (three panel) brochure. You will want it to fold and fit easily into a #10 envelope. The terms *flier* and *brochure* are often used interchangeably, but basically a flier (sometimes spelled flyer) is a single sheet with a simple message, while a brochure contains several folded panels and contains more detailed information. This becomes your single most important piece of literature in your marketing campaign. It must answer all of the questions that might pop into a prospective buyer's mind. It both describes the book fully and talks about you, the qualified author, as an expert in your field. Use your endorsements, testimonials, and positive reviews liberally. This is the opportunity for you to toot your own horn.

A memorable and productive brochure or flier will continue telling book buyers, pastors, convention directors, associates, and new networking clients your story after you've made initial contact with them. Make sure it demonstrates the most salable qualities of your message and of you as author.

For maximum impact, print your flier on eye-catching paper (like fluorescent yellow, orange, or green), design it to communicate the point you want to make, and distribute it in places frequented by your target audience. For your brochure, you'll want to select a colored paper stock with possibly a colored ink. This will give the appearance of a quality two-color piece that is both attractive and well-produced.

Your brochure and your business card should go into everything you mail, including every book you send out. Keep them in your car. Hand them out everywhere you go. These become pass-a-longs to others when your readers are asked, "Where can I get a copy of that book?"

Another common industry practice is to use your book jacket or book cover to create your promotional brochure. The outside is already colorful and eye-catching, the inside allows you room to print all the other pertinent details and ordering information. If you order overruns of the cover when you place your book order, the additional cost is nominal. Some companies print the press release on the back of the book jacket, others accompany a book jacket mailing with a separate press release.

Printed Postcards

Printed postcards are becoming an industry staple for advertising. This economical, eye-catching format requires less postage and no time-consuming stuffing of envelopes. Make sure your postcard includes ordering information, and send it to all your friends, relatives, and colleagues who might order a book. When you design your postcard or any PR materials, stress the benefits of the book's contents.

> *You must immediately pull the reader in, and your appeal must get an emotional response that makes him want to do something—like buy your book.*

Direct mail advertising may be especially helpful if you are trying to reach a large number of friends, relatives, fellow writers, area bookstores. These days even major publishing houses are using direct mail postcards to announce an author's new book. Make sure your postcard is colorful, catchy, convincing, and has all the pertinent ordering information.

If you are going to do several large mailings (over 200 each), then you may want to purchase a bulk mailing permit from the post office. As in all direct mail marketing, it takes a number of mailings before the consumer says to himself, "Yeah, I need to get that book." Remember two key words when designing your direct-marketing piece or promotional package: *pull* and *appeal*. You must immediately pull the reader in, and your appeal must get an emotional response that makes him want to do something—like buy your book.

Use your entire mailing list frequently in order to keep your address corrections current and to keep your name in front of your customers. Make sure you add those collected business cards gathered at fairs and exhibits, and the roster of attendees at workshops to your mailing list at your earliest opportunity. It takes that combination of networking, publicity, word-of-mouth advertising, speaking, regular direct mailings, newsletter, and other free publicity opportunities (articles, news releases) to build a successful self-publishing business.

Self-publishing guru Dan Poynter in *The Self-Publishing Manual* says, "We firmly believe the best way to sell most nonfiction books is with book reviews, news releases, and a limited amount of highly targeted direct mail."

It is generally believed that a book advertised by direct mail will produce a return of around 2 percent. Of course, the better your mailing list and the more attractive and convincing your mailing piece, the greater your return orders will be. Also, the more you personalize your mailings, the more specific you will become in interesting your readers. Remember, a direct mail advertising followed by telephone calls to your key contacts can become your most cost-effective method of advertising.

Press Release

The best way to alert print and broadcast editors about your book is with a professional news release. The news director will look twice at a news release that has an angle or reason that is uniquely important to his publication or radio/television station. Finding these reasons or angles is the best way to obtain the "free" advertising you need to start creating the buzz.

Press Releases are always timed for the release date or shortly before. The ideal press release serves both to announce your book and to whet the reader's appetite for your new title. Answer the question, "What's in it for me?" Stress an angle that reveals the book as important and timely. Try to reveal human interest, relevancy, and humor. Whenever possible, tie your book in with a current event or news story. Include brief information about you as to background, experience, reason, and credentials for writing the book.

A provocative headline with a fast-paced anecdote that tells the story behind the book is the bread and butter of harried book review editors. Make sure that your press release creates excitement and a desire for the reader to know more. If you have several different identifiable audiences, you may need to create various opening paragraphs designed to "hook" that particular audience. Of course, the most important information answers the question, "Where can I obtain a copy of the book?" This could be from a bookstore, from you, or from your distributor.

When you are writing your press release, think like an editor. How will the editor be able to use this material? If your press release sounds simply like a straightforward sales pitch for your new book, it will probably be tossed in the wastebasket. If, on the other hand, your press release offers solid information that the editor's readers will find interesting or useful, then your chances are much greater for grabbing the free publicity.

Your list of where to send a press release should include the alumni publications of all the schools you attended, newspapers of all the cities you've lived in, magazines that cover news related to your book topic, and organizations interested in the subject of your book.

The self-published author's best ally may be the local or regional newspaper. When regional interest begins to build, it often leads to radio and television interviews. This kind of attention eventually alerts bigger media and also major publishers. Reviews and news stories, even in small local outlets, often lead to big things for the well-written book. Stories abound of self-published books that went on to become best-selling titles either before or after they were picked up by major publishing houses.

The Press Release Primer

Make sure it's news, stick to the point, and do your homework. The less work an editor has to do on a press release, the better its chances are of getting published.

• Format Notes

Use your own letterhead. This will include your phone, fax, and e-mail numbers so you can be contacted quickly if more information is needed. A press release should always be dated. Remember, this is supposed to be news. You want to give editors a sense of timeliness and urgency, and also let them know when to call to do a follow-up. A release should always be double-spaced, so the editor can easily make changes. Keep releases to a maximum of two pages—that should present enough information for a short article or generate enough curiosity to get your phone ringing.

The name at the top of the release should be yours or that of the person you want contacted. It should be someone who is fully informed about every aspect of the news release and who will drop everything to get the editors what they need for their story angle.

Names mentioned within the body of the copy or at the bottom are those of people you hope will be quoted or mentioned if your story gets into print—they are not intended to be primary contacts.

• Make Sure It's News

Make sure your headline reads like a *news* item and gives the editor a story hook.

Not: *Publisher Introduces New Book on Self-Publishing*
Better: *New Sure-Sale PR Help for the Self-Publishing Author*

It never hurts to use the word *new*. This way the editor has to read on to find out about "the new sure-sale help."

• Keep to the Point

Don't bury the lead. Make sure the most important and useful information is delivered right up front. Don't try to cover the world in a press release. If editors want more information, they'll call. As a rule, try to keep product and company names to a minimum. Don't worry, if an article gets written, your company will get mentioned by virtue of the fact that it's the source of the news.

• Emphasize Benefits

Don't tell about the features of a book, product, or service—tell about the benefits. This is the most common mistake in public relations. You want the copy to get right into how effective the new PR tools are to use or what problems

they solve for self-publishing authors. This is also more difficult to write than simply listing a book's features. It sounds
obvious, but never let a press release go out unless you're
sure the facts are straight.

• Prep Work and Follow-Up

Good public relations is about serving the editor's interest as much as your own. Build a rapport with editors.
Become a key source of information about the industry—not
just about your company—for editors. In turn, use them as
sounding boards for things you're doing in product development and in your company in general. About a week
before sending a release, tell the editors you are sending it
and ask who should receive it. Follow-up is where the rub-
ber meets the road. Set dates for making phone calls.
Remember, the more of the editor's job you can do, the
higher your chances of getting an article into print.

Media Kit—Also Called Publicity Packet

A good media kit is a snappy presentation folder containing: a synopsis/back cover copy of the book, a good
reproducible photo of the book front cover, a black and
white photo of the author, and your author bio sketch. A
media kit is essential if you are going to compete with the big
boys for article space and radio or TV talk shows or interviews. Information to include in your media kits are: a one-
page press release, fact sheet, prepared questions that you
could be asked in an interview, book information sheet, one-
page book flier, acknowledgment card, endorsements, complimentary comments from readers, impressive reviews from
any authorities, reprints of clippings, copies of articles you

have written and published related to your book topic, and any other pertinent material.

MEDIA KIT CHECKLIST

- ❏ cover
- ❏ synopsis or back cover copy of the book
- ❏ good reproducible photo of book jacket
- ❏ author bio sketch
- ❏ black and white photo of author
- ❏ one-page press release
- ❏ prepared interview questions
- ❏ book information fact sheet
- ❏ one-page book flier or brochure
- ❏ reply acknowledgment card
- ❏ endorsements page
- ❏ complimentary comments from readers
- ❏ impressive reviews from any authorities
- ❏ newspaper clippings
- ❏ copies of published articles
- ❏ review copy of book or excerpts

A great book review is a dynamite marketing tool. As your collection of reviews grow, add them to the kit, circulate them to local media, bookstores, distributors, anyone who might be able to move your book along or make a quantity purchase.

Your author bio sketch can be a paragraph or two, up to one complete page, describing who you are and your accomplishments. Don't be confused here. A vita or resume is not a bio. The two are quite different. According to best-selling author Dottie Walters in *Speak and Grow Rich*, "A vita lists

AUTHOR BIOGRAPHICAL SKETCH

Elaine Wright Colvin is a market specialist, editor, and career consultant for writers/publishers wanting to keep in touch with the changing trends and needs of the Christian writing industry. In 1983 she founded Writers Information Network ... The Professional Association for Christian Writers, for which she publishes the WIN-INFORMER *newsletter.*

She has directed Writers Conferences and spoken at more than 150 workshops, conventions, Elderhostels, university classes, conferences, and retreats nationwide. She has published hundreds of articles, poems, devotions, and book reviews. She is author, co-author, contributing author, or consultant on more than 35 published books. Her first book was The Religious Writers Marketplace *(Running Press, 1980). Her most recent,* Treasury of God's Virtues, *August 1998 (now in its third printing), is one of the fastest-selling books of Publications International. Elaine has been an Associate Member of the Evangelical Press Association and a CBA Media Team member since 1980. She is listed in* Contemporary Authors, Volume 106. *Her awards include: Best Writer's Helps Award at the 1981 Mount Hermon Christian Writers Conference, Outstanding Motivator of Christian Writers Award at the 1984 Warm Beach Christian Writers Conference, and a Special Recognition Award at the 20th annual Mount Hermon Christian Writers Conference in 1989.*

the educational background of the speaker and may be several pages long. A bio is one sheet. It lists the reasons this speaker is an authority on this subject." Radio and television program producers, conference and meeting planners just want facts about your qualifications to speak on your topic. "If you've written articles or books, spoken for major companies, or been presented with honors, these are the things you should list in your bio," according to Walters. Occasionally you'll be asked to supply a few biographical lines for the editor's page of a magazine, or as a photo cut line. Then you'll only want to include a thought or two relating to how you discovered or developed the subject of your book.

Your media presentation kit is something that will be used, adapted, and specialized over the years. You won't be able to afford to send a complete media packet to every radio/TV/newspaper contact you make—so be selective. Radio broadcasts make good use of media kits, where most print media do just as well with a quality press release. A publicity packet that can go to the people featuring you for autograph parties and signings is always a good idea. It does not have to be as thorough as the media kit—so pick and choose those items most appropriate for the situation.

Galleys and Review Copies

Some publications will review only galley proofs and others review only finished books. Many publications require a galley ninety days prior to the publishing release date. An announcement flier (also called advance book info form) asking whether a galley or finished book is preferred by the periodicals/publications appropriate for your book is a good way to say "heads up" and to save yourself both time and money.

A galley is a bound draft of your book (usually a spiral bound photocopy) that you can send for endorsements and review months before your book is due for publication. If book galleys are not ready in time to meet the deadline of the periodicals you are targeting, then it is acceptable to bind and send out copies of your edited manuscript instead. You will want to make sure they are marked "Uncorrected Proof. Do not use for official quotations without checking with the author."

All galleys sent out for review must contain a front page of pertinent data: title, author, author bio, publication date, price, classification, ISBN, number of pages, and number of illustrations.

Mailing large quantities of books can become a headache if you don't have a prearranged plan. Check out the service providers in your community to determine who can best fit your needs: UPS, FedEx, USPS, etc. Find out how much insurance comes automatically with your shipments and determine if this is adequate for your quantities.

When mailing actual review copies of the book itself, include a news release and other promotional materials (i.e. author bio, media questions, price, and ordering information).

Many publicists recommend doing a follow-up phone call to inquire if the review copy was received and to jog the editor's/broadcaster's memory. When you can include a small gift or practical item with the press kit, it adds the incentive of moving your book to the top of the pile. Anything that draws positive attention to your book is worth extra effort and expense.

After the book review has been published it is smart to remember that even book reviewers appreciate handwritten thank-you notes—and especially when the review has generated a good response.

ESSENCE PUBLISHING
Uncorrected Proof

TITLE: *A Savvy Approach to Book Sales*
SUBTITLE: *Marketing Advice to Get the Buzz Going*
AUTHOR: *Elaine Wright Colvin*
PRICE/PAGES/BINDING: *$9.95US/140 pp/Softcover*
BOOK ISBN: *1-55306-105-5*
CATEGORY: *Reference/Writing*
SCHEDULED RELEASE DATE: *April 2000*

BRIEF: The biggest job an author faces is book promotion. If you, the author, are not out there trying to make your book stand out, you will simply be lost in the crowd of 150,000 plus other new books that roll off the presses each year. There are more than 1.3 million books in print. How will you get the attention your book needs to jump start sales and create the exciting buzz? You are the one who can make it happen. You are the one who can tout the benefits and create eager waiting readers. If you are feeling slightly timid and overwhelmed, here is the help you need. Step-by-step ideas and concrete samples will help you set your plan of action in motion.

AUTHOR BIO: Elaine Wright Colvin is a market specialist, editor, and career consultant for writers/publishers wanting to keep in touch with the changing trends and needs of the Christian writing industry. She is founder and director of Writers Information Network ... The Professional Association for Christian Writers. She is publisher of the bimonthly newsletter, the *WIN-INFORMER*.

This bound galley is sent to help you review the book and schedule a printed review in your publication or on-the-air. Editorial changes will still be made in this proof copy before the book is published. If any material from the book is to be quoted in a review, the quotation should be checked against the finished book.

All excerpts must receive permission before they are published; direct your requests in writing to Essence Publishing Subsidiary Rights and Permission Department at the address below or by fax to: (613) 962-3055.

Please give proper attribution (title, author, publisher, copyright date) in all references to Essence books. Whenever you review or refer to a Essence book in your periodical or on your stations, please send a tear sheet or script and the date it was published or aired to Essence Media Relations at the address below. Thank you.

Essence Publishing
44 Moira Street West
Belleville, Ontario, Canada K8P 1S3
1-800-238-6375 • (613) 962-3294

BOOK PROMOTION "TO DO" LIST

- ❏ create marketing plan
- ❏ update author bio
- ❏ write book synopsis/description
- ❏ write fact information sheet
- ❏ compile media list for book galleys
- ❏ compile media list for press releases

- ❏ compile list to receive review books
- ❏ compile direct mail list of friends, relatives, associates, etc.
- ❏ solicit endorsements
- ❏ write cover letter to send with galleys
- ❏ design flier and/or brochure
- ❏ have professional PR photo taken
- ❏ write press release
- ❏ decide about hiring a publicist
- ❏ secure a distributor or put a fulfillment plan in place
- ❏ write and submit magazine articles
- ❏ send galley copies
- ❏ send pre-publication announcements
- ❏ design and print extra PR materials: postcards, bookmarks, T-shirts, pens, etc.
- ❏ mail review copies
- ❏ schedule media interviews
- ❏ secure speaking engagements
- ❏ plan launch party
- ❏ create book signing opportunities
- ❏ compile endorsement page and quote review page
- ❏ work on news and feature write-ups for press
- ❏ contact local newspaper columnists and community newspapers
- ❏ collect samples of other authors' PR pieces
- ❏ take another self-published author to coffee

THREE

Why You Need a Niche Market

The change in the publishing industry that has had the greatest impact on writers is the trend known as narrowcasting—publishing for definable niche market segments rather than for a mass audience.

A niche is any small position or "hole" in the marketplace—unfilled or filled poorly by a competitor.

The most logical place to start in your book marketing efforts is with the special interest audiences. Those readers are the most likely to buy it, get excited about it, and then tell their friends. Once you get "word-of-mouth" going among your target market audience, you hope and pray that it will have a ripple effect to larger audiences.

Several years ago in his best-selling book, *Megatrends*, John Naisbitt wrote: "In a relatively short time, the unified mass society has fractionalized into many diverse groups of people with a wide array of differing tastes and values, what advertisers call a market-segmented, market-decentralized society. This fact has tremendous influence on trade books as well as magazine publishing today."

Creating Consumer Demand

"Who will buy your book?" is the fundamental question every author and book publisher asks. It is important for an author to define their niche, specialize in it, and become known as the "expert" in a particular area. This is especially true when you hope to write and publish several books. When you know the answer to this all-encompassing question, you're ready to go on to the next big question.

Where Will Your Book Be Shelved?

Assuming at least some bookstores will carry your book, where will it be shelved? What subject category does it naturally fall under? What books do you find on these shelves now that will be your competition? What are their prices and book sizes? What can you give your book title or subtitle that will make it stand out from the crowd? Be realistic and objective. This book is no longer an integral part of your self, but has become a product that must be marketed to the masses.

Besides Christian, independent, and chain bookstores, what specialty shops, boutiques, sporting good stores, gift shops, nurseries/gardens, tea shops, coffee houses, children's stores, airport or hotel gift shops, novelty stores, or other places would be a natural outlet for your product?

WHERE WILL YOUR BOOK BE SHELVED?
ECPA Designated Book Categories

Academic
Bibles
Bible Study
Biography/
    Autobiography
Charismatic
Youth/Children
    Activity Books
    Board Books
    Bible Reference
    Bible Story Books
    Chapter Books Fiction
    Chapter Non-Fiction
    Coloring Books
    Devotional
    Educational
    Learn to Read
    Book with Music
    Picture Books
    Pre-School
Youth Interests
    College
    Dating/Sex
    Devotions
    Teen Fiction
    Seasonal
    Baptism
    Easter
    First Communion
    Christmas

Christian Living
    Aging
    Biography
    Charismatic
    Career
    Classics
    Discipleship
    Decisions
    Encouragement
    Faith
    Forgiveness
    Healing
    Personal Worship
    Revival
    Spiritual Growth
Family Concerns
    Fathering
    Homeschooling
    Mothering
    Parenting
    Sex Education
Personal Finance
General Interest
    Business
    Cookbooks
    Crafts
    Diet and Health
    Friendship
    Humor
    Puzzle Books

Sports
Tracts/Booklets
Gift/Seasonal
  Mini Books
  Journals
  Photo Albums
  Advent
  Calendars
  Easter
  Fathers
  Graduation
  Lent
  Mothers
  Thanksgiving
  Valentine's Day
  Christmas
  Birth
  Birthday
  Get Well
  Wedding
Issues
  African-American
  Politics
  Science and Faith
  Social Issues
Love and Marriage
  Divorce
  Marriage
  Difficulties
  Marriage Growth
  Preparedness
  Relationships
  Dating

Sexuality
  Wedding Planners
Miscellaneous
Men
New Believer
Psychology
  Grief
  Consolation
  Lay Counseling
  Recovery
Seniors
Single Living
Women
Fiction
  Allegory
  Fantasy
  Science Fiction
  Classic
  Historical
  Romance
  Western
  Suspense
  Mystery
  General
  Contemporary
Literature and the Arts
  Art
  Essays/Memoirs
  Music
  Poetry
  Short Stories
Spiritual Life
  Contemplative Life

Inspirational
Prayer and Devotional
Spiritual Warfare
Children's Churchtime Programs
Classroom Resources
Director Helps and Resources
Undated Curriculum
Day and Homeschool Curriculum
Sunday School Curriculum
Youth Ministry Resources

[This partial list is reprinted by permission of Doug Ross, president/CEO of Evangelical Christian Publishers Association (ECPA), 1969 East Broadway Road, Suite 2, Tempe, AZ 85282. The complete list is available on the Web site: www.ecpa.org or by sending an SASE to the ECPA office.]

Where Can You Speak? Teach? Appear?

Start now to identify all of the parts of your book that would make good presentations. Do some serious brainstorming on where these talks should be held and how to get your promo information into the hands of the individuals that do the inviting. When you know WHERE you'd like to go, you'll be ready to send out your brochures and media kits in an effort to secure those all important invitations.

Consider what the subject of your talk would be if you were to speak at: a library, retirement community, school, college or university, Rotary Club, Kiwanis, Christian Women's Club, Aglow meeting, Association, retreat, bookstore, MOPS, workshop, museum, Welcome Wagon luncheon, Bible Study group, etc. Read the club/group meeting announcements in your area newspapers to remind yourself of all the opportunities in your own backyard.

In your PR cover letters, when seeking speaking engagements, be sure to establish the needs/benefits quotient. Start with the useful and then go on to the fun parts of your book—this is what will keep your audience clamoring for more. By emphasizing the strengths of your book, you can answer the "what's in it for me?" question. Once you convince groups that your talk/theme is just right for their audience, then you need to convince them of your special abilities as a speaker or entertainer. Visual aids, slide/video presentations, charts, graphs, all help make your talk effective and memorable.

Does your book lend itself as a textbook in an adult education class, a community college, a group reading/study club or some other type of situation? Teaching, with all the natural PR associated with forming new classes, is an excellent way to get extended publicity. This is basically a no-risk way to supplement your income while waiting for money from sales to come in. The downside of a three-month or more teaching commitment is that you won't be able to leave town for long, should other more lucrative opportunities present themselves. With the right topic, you might prefer the entrepreneurial approach, where you offer a workshop or seminar. But in putting on workshops, you bear all the risk and work of financing and promoting them yourself.

Every speaking engagement should be an opportunity for back-of-room sales, also sometimes called "selling products from the platform." Never devote more than a few minutes to "selling from the platform." When you spend too much time describing your products, your listeners may become resentful; they didn't pay to hear a commercial. But when your presentation is good, people will want to hear more. The key for successful speakers is matching your

JEANNIE SATRE

Sometimes, when you're generous at giving away your books, like Jeannie Satre is, the speaking invitations just come to you. In one hurried e-mail to the WIN office last spring, Jeannie, author of *Eight Was Not Enough ... The Unlikely Adventures of an Only Child* (ACW Press, 1998), wrote: "I've spoken at Kiwanis in Berkeley and next week at Soroptimist in Concord, CA. (I've never solicited 'speaks.') And today the Soroptimist Chair called to say that I have been one of four women chosen to receive their 'Women of Distinction Award.' I told you that I'm speaking at Mount Hermon's 'Women at Change Point' Conference in May. My book will be part of the book reviews and available at Mount Hermon bookstore. Also...serendipity...on my trip to Israel, the owner of the gift shop on the Sea of Galilee said she'd buy fifteen of my books as a test. They will be at the Sea of Galilee and the Dead Sea. Neat, huh?"

Jeannie and her dentist husband, Neal, have dedicated their lives to raising special children from around the world. Twin boys born to them were followed by girls from Korea, children from Mother Teresa's orphanage in India, and a girl from Walnut Creek. "This is an intensely personal story about faith and family. If you are like me, your heart will be touched, inspired and challenged to reach out to the world in ways you never before allowed yourself to imagine," wrote well-known author and speaker Colleen Townsend Evans in an endorsement. (Jeannie Satre, 180 Shady Lane, Walnut Creek CA 94596; $11.00, plus $3 shipping.)

presentation style and the content of your talks to your audience in such a way that they are demanding to hear more. At the end of the meeting, your books, audio cassettes, videotapes, training materials, and other items will be in demand and may create lucrative back-of-room sales income.

Wherever you go to speak, take (or ship ahead) enough books, tapes, and other product to sell at the speaker's table at the back of the room. Also, you'll want to have a good supply of your book order forms, business cards, brochures, bookmarks, and promotional material with you. Always have the MC announce your availability to autograph books and answer questions at your book table after the meeting.

Tips from Speakers Who Sell at Meetings

- always refer to your sales table as the autograph table; not the table in the back

- try to locate the book table in a heavy traffic area (between the exit, refreshments, and bathroom)

- put an enlarged photograph of yourself and your book on easels or self-standing signs on your table

- be prepared with a large piece of colorful felt or knit cloth to cover your table in case something suitable is not provided

- stack your products to make an attractive display and store all extra supplies out of sight under the table

- always have trained sales table assistants with you to make change and handle the sales. This will free you up to talk to your customers and sign autographs.

Be careful about offering to speak for nothing—if you can just have a book table. Unless you know the group well and can be guaranteed a very big crowd, you could end up very disappointed. When you have to drive several hours, spend time in preparation for your talks, and end up with a small group and only a couple of sales, you will wonder if it was worth it. It is best to have some kind of speaker's fee and to expect that your travel costs will be covered. But when the crowd is good, and your topic right on, many authors have found that "back-of-the-room sales" can generate even more money than the speaking fee.

If you lack confidence in your speaking abilities, there are a number of books available with practical suggestions for writing and delivering a good speech.

Books for Developing Better Speaking

Who, Me, Give a Speech? Handbook for Christian Women, Nancy I. Alford, Baker Book House, 1987, $7.95.

How to Talk So People Will Listen, Steve Brown, Baker Book House, 1993. "Nobody ever gave a good speech without being afraid. That fear, when channeled properly, will be the very thing that will create an effective speech."

Better Speeches in TEN Simple Steps, James W. Robinson, Prima Publishing, 1995, $9.95. Even if you have to give a speech tomorrow, you'll benefit from knowing how to: avoid the #1 mistake in public speaking; overcome stage fright; use humor—and how not to; determine the perfect length for any speech; keep it simple; create a fireworks finale; plus what to do when things go wrong, and much more.

Public Speaking: A Handbook for Christians, Second Edition, Duane Litfin, Baker Book House, 1995. This book will help build your self-confidence as you learn practical how-to-do-it steps. In a humorous, interesting, and comprehensive manner, the authors takes the reader through the process of preparing speeches for both religious and non-religious settings.

The Complete Guide to Christian Writing and Speaking, edited by Susan Titus Osborn, Promise Publishing, Orange, CA, 1994. The chapter "The Business Side of Speaking" holds practical suggestions to help your speaking ministry run smoothing. Topics include: promoting yourself, ministry information sheet, contact sheet, contract, speaking fees, clothing choices, visual aids, handouts, book table, and record keeping.

Speak Up With Confidence. A step-by-step guide to successful public speaking, Carol Kent, Nelson, 1987, $12.95. Contains helpful hints on preparing a great speech, overcoming stage fright, giving your personal testimony effectively, leading discussions groups, and more.

The Christian Communicator's Handbook. A guide to help you make the message plain, Dr. Tom Nash, Victor, 1995. Helpful chapters include: Choose Appropriate Media; Improve Your One-on-One Communications Skills; Use the Best of Both Mass and Interpersonal Communication; Understand How New Ideas Spread.

MARILYN JORDAN GEORGE

Marilyn Jordan George has found her book lends itself to all kinds of speaking opportunities. *Following the Alaskan Dream ... My Salmon Trolling Adventures in the Last Frontier* contains lively adventures that have kept her speaking at bookstores, Alaska Press Women, Elderhostels, retirement communities, radio talk shows, museums, and more. She regales her audiences with a lively telling of "Let Me Go Back to Where the Cement Grows." Now past her 75th birthday, she fills her schedule with traveling, and before each stop (in Iowa, Idaho, Washington, Oregon, and Alaska) she has done her homework to find appropriate speaking, newspaper and/or radio interviews, and book signing opportunities. In less than a year, Marilyn had to go back for a second printing, and the third "back to press" is expected soon as she's down to her last 100 copies. (Order from Marilyn George, PO Box 1031, Petersburg AK 99833. $24.95, plus $4 shipping.)

FOUR

Hurdles You'll Need to Jump

Yuou've got a great book, it's getting rave reviews, you've fielded a few radio interviews—so what's the problem? The problem is that the readers whose interest you've captured can't find your book. It doesn't seem to be available in any of the local stores. This is when you must remember that having good distribution outlets is just as important as getting those book reviews and feature stories.

Many authors believe that they can do it all—publish, promote, and distribute without outside help. Perhaps they can. But of major importance are getting a toll-free phone number, setting up to accept credit card payments, and processing orders for quick turn-around. When you hear it put that way, you may want to consider the alternatives.

Approaching Distributors

Distributors are generally considered your one big link in achieving high volume sales and getting your books into the major bookstores. A distributor's sales force can promote your book in places where you can't go (like to the major wholesalers). Distributors do some kind of marketing of the books they carry and so they are selective based on what they think they can sell. Distributors publish their own catalogs with synopses or reviews designed to promote the books.

Wholesalers can also promote your book, but most of them do it simply through a catalog and do not have a sales force. Most wholesalers are strictly fulfillment houses. They are order takers—the middleman between the publisher and the store or customers. They do not create sales—they fill the demand that someone else creates. Many wholesalers have a regional distribution territory. To get a better understanding of the comprehensive coverage of distributors and wholesalers, read the *Literary Marketplace* at your library. It is easier to get both wholesalers and distributors excited about a book that is being publicized and promoted. But even securing the aid of a distribution house will not guarantee sales. Your best chance may be to find a company that successfully sells books similar to yours.

Seller beware—selling books through distributors and wholesalers means it can be a long time before you see any cash in your pocket. The distributor must sell your book to a wholesaler or bookstore, who must sell to their customer... and you don't get paid until the customer pays the bookstore and the money goes up the line again. At each step there could be as much as a 30 to 45-day wait for money to change hands, thus a three to six-month delay in your receiving payment. And, of course, there is no guarantee the

ABOUT DICK SLEEPER DISTRIBUTION

As a part of our goal to give the "little guy" access into the marketplace and to make available to the public good books they might otherwise never know about, we combine the publications of a number of small publishers and self-publishers into a single catalog and solicit and fill orders from Christian retailers and wholesalers. We produce two catalogs and order forms each year: at the beginning of each calendar year and in early summer. These comply with the established rhythms of the publishing industry. It is more difficult for us to add books to our list between these times. We also exhibit and take orders at the CBA (Christian Booksellers Association) conventions in July and January. We do, on occasion, also exhibit at other conventions and meetings and give our clients an opportunity to participate in those events.

books will ever be sold, in which case you will receive no payment. You place your books with distributors "on consignment." Beware of giving any distributor an exclusive unless you are convinced that they cover all the book trade you need to reach. The "Contract with Book Distributor" and checklists offered in *Business and Legal Forms* (Tad Crawford) can be very helpful to you in negotiating this process.

One more caution: Distributors demand and get big discounts for handling your book which will drastically cut into your profit margin if you have not priced it to take into account these discounts. With the shrinking profit margins for distributors, many are adding deep discounting, service charges, increased cash reserves, and fees for unsalable returns to their contracts. New self-publishers are often surprised to find that distributors and wholesalers expect discounts of 55-65 percent.

When thinking about the cover price of your book, an often-used rule of thumb is that your book should be priced at five times the cost of having it printed. Dan Poynter says you must price your book at eight times production cost. "Without a sufficient price, there is not enough money for promotion, and without promotion, a book won't sell. If the book fails to sell, there is no money for promotion or even to pay the print bill. You must assume that 98 percent of your books will be sold at wholesale prices" (*For All the Right Reasons,* p. 273). Double-check and see if this is what the market will bear on your book. In today's economy, with the big discount department stores all being in the book business, it's a reality that if you want to sell a lot of books, you will have to keep the price down.

In considering who to use for fulfillment services and whether or not to solicit the help of a distributor, you will want to closely look at the responsibilities and services the distributor is offering.

> How will they help in the promotion of your book?
>
> Who will bear the expenses?
>
> Will the distributor do more than place the book in its catalog?
>
> What discount do they require from you?
>
> What are their terms of payment?
>
> How big of a territory do they cover?
>
> What is their success record with your genre?
>
> What is their reputation in the industry?

Do they have booths at the major trade shows or do any advertising in appropriate media?

Who supplies the press releases and review copies and pays the cost of distributing them?

Too many authors have hung their head saying, "I had a few good-sized distributors, but with no publicity there was no interest and no sales to the bookstores." Explore every possible way to get your book into the Baker & Taylor, Spring Arbor, Ingram, Appalachian, and Amazon.com computer systems. These are the main ordering sources for most bookstores.

In an editorial in *Small Press* magazine, Mardi Link wrote: "When it comes to signing with a national distributor, many publishers are drowned in lost sales if they don't, drowned in fees, returns, and questionable profits if they do. Neither independent publishers, bookstores, distributors, nor the almighty marketplace has come up with a solution to how books can be sold nationally and still make a respectable profit for all concerned" (*Small Press,* May/June 1997).

If you are still having problems coming up with the right distribution method for your book, go to your public library. In the reference section, you should find the book *The American Book Trade Directory.* Here you will find more than 1200 wholesalers and distributors listed with a description of their subject interest.

Make a list of a dozen or more distributors that could be a possible fit with your book and then call to ask about their submission procedure. Be realistic—just because you apply to a distributor does not mean your book will be accepted. Your book title stands against stiff competition even for distributors and will be evaluated on the size of the print run, writing quality, subject matter, promotional campaigns, and packaging. Plus, someone makes a guess as to whether or not they think your book will sell based on the competition with similar books already in the marketplace.

Be creative in convincing a distributor that you have a great book and that you are going to be aggressively promoting your book to make sure it sells.

Book Distributors and Wholesalers Serving the Christian Market

Appalachian, Inc.
P.O. Box 1573
506 Princeton Rd.
Johnson City TN 37601
1-800-289-2772

Baker & Taylor Company
652 East Main St.
PO Box 6920
Bridgewater NJ 08807-0920
(201) 218-0400

Book World Services, Inc.
1230 Heil Quaker Blvd.
LaVergne TN 37086
(to the general trade)

Christian Distribution Services (CDS)
1230 Heil Quaker Blvd.
LaVergne TN 37086
(615) 793-5955; e-mail: cds@minister.com
(Exclusive full-service distributor to the CBA market for small publishers with at least five titles or a single title with a

dynamic sales history; an extension of the publisher offering a sales and marketing team.)

Ingram Book Company
One Ingram Blvd.
PO Box 3006
LaVergne TN 37086-1986
(615) 793-5000

New Day Christian Distributors
126 Shivel Dr.
Hendersonville TN 37075
1-800-251-3633

Riverside Distributors
PO Box 370
1500 Riverside Dr.
Iowa Falls IA 50126-0370
(515) 648-4271

Dick Sleeper Distribution
18680-B Langensand Rd.
Sandy OR 97055-9427
(503) 668-3454; FAX: (503) 668-5313
e-mail: SleepyDick@Bigfoot.com

Spring Arbor Distributors
10885 Textile Rd.
Belleville MI 48111
1-800-395-5599; (313) 481-0900
www.springarbor.com
(to the CBA market)

Successful Living Book Distribution
4050 Lee Vance View
Colorado Springs CO 80936-3665
(719) 535-0318

Whitaker Distributors
30 Hunt Valley Circle
New Kinsington PA 15608
(412) 334-7000

Making Friends with the Gatekeepers

Does your book have a title that says, "Grab me, read me," as the customer walks by the shelf in the bookstore? Unless you can convince bookstore owners/buyers that they have a vast audience of potential readers who want to have your book, you may have a hard time getting it onto their bookstore shelves. Your title and subtitle, your cover, your theme, and your promise must all make readers want to grab your book and skim through the pages to see what you've done. And it takes a good deal of self-promotion to get those readers into the store looking for your book in the first place.

Bookstore owners are not necessarily persuaded by distributors, wholesalers, publishers, or even authors to stock books for a long time. Book shelf-life is quite short—three to six months—if a book is not selling. They can't afford to have dead books on their shelves. Here again, you are the one who must make readers buy your book. As is often said, it is important to remember: "Bookstores don't sell books, authors do!" Every author soon learns that without aggressive promoting, books sold on consignment in bookstores may end up gathering dust, and unsold copies will eventually have to be picked up. The best method for motivating bookstores to actively stock your book is through customer pressure. Get your friends, relatives, and fans into the stores requesting your book. This will help create a demand.

The best bookstore outlet for self-publishers is the independent non-chain store. Buyers at the independents don't have to abide by corporate rules, and they can be more receptive to local authors. When you first set out to make cold sales calls on bookstores, it may seem a little overwhelming. But don't let that stop you. Remember, you believe in your product and you believe in your message! Your talks with bookstore buyers will probably go quite smoothly. You will show them your book, let them feel it as you describe the best features for your intended readers.

> *Have a sixty-second (one or two liner) "handle" giving the theme and benefit ready to roll off your tongue the moment you're asked, "Well, so what's this book all about?"*

Be prepared. Have a sixty-second (one or two liner) "handle" giving the theme and benefit ready to roll off your tongue the moment you're asked, "Well, so what's this book all about?" That is all the time you may have before a customer or a phone call interrupts your sales pitch. Stress the advantages and benefits of your book over the competition if you've written in a topic area that seems to be particularly crowded. If there are special features that tie in to your locale or target audience, be ready to offer proof to back up your claims.

Then be ready to give them an offer they can't refuse—a special discount price for a cash sale on two to five trial copies in their store. (Or work out what is appropriate for your product and the size/type of store you are presenting it to.) Bookstores are used to ordering books at 40-60 percent discounts and not paying until the book actually sells (or they return it to you). It may take some fancy talking to try and get payment up front, but this should always be your goal. Placing books on consignment is a second best way to go.

Remember, your presentation should be very short and to the point. Storekeepers are very busy people and not particularly fond of unannounced salesmen. However, if you can keep them talking and interested and asking you questions about your book, you just may have them "hooked."

Don't be afraid to be quiet. Books require silence for quick reads and perusals. After all, your bookstore owner/manager has his shelves full of hundreds, even thousands of books. Therefore, he is probably a speed reader and a quick assessor of whether or not your product would be something that would sell well in his store. But he needs a few moments to look over your book and come to his decision. During this time, silence is golden.

You may not always be fortunate enough to find the person who has the "final say/purchasing power" in the store when you make your first cold call. This is when you must be certain to have a media kit/brochure/business card or other pertinent material, with all the appropriate ordering information (designed specifically for bookstores), to leave. Be sure to get the correct name and spelling of the person you should be talking to—the book buyer. If you don't hear back from the book buyer in a week, make your follow-up call.

You can also do a lot of networking with booksellers from around the country by attending Booksellers Conventions. There is the CBA Convention held in various locations in July, as well as the CBA Expo held in January. These are announced in *CBA Marketplace* magazine. The American Booksellers Association has regional conventions that are advertised well in advance in *Publishers Weekly*. Unless you are with a distributor or major publisher, you will not be allowed to "sell" books on the exhibition floors, but there is certainly nothing to keep you from networking and exchanging business cards (and handing them your brochure) with all of the booksellers you meet. Adding these names and addresses to your database will give your mailing list extra potential. Be sure to send a follow-up PR postcard or other mailing soon after the convention.

Creating Author Signing Opportunities

"There is no substitute for the face-to-face interaction that comes from visiting stores and greeting an audience," says children's author Mary Manz Simon. "I love getting to visit bookstores. I call it 'author's gratification'—meeting my readers and bantering with them about my books" (*Christian Retailing*, March 18, 1999).

Author signings work great in both a party/festive atmosphere or an educational/book seminar setting. They may be given by your club or association, church, community, friends, local Christian bookstore, or Barnes & Noble. The key to a successful signing and selling opportunity is lots of publicity. Make sure that newspapers, bulletins, and newsletters get the date and pertinent information well in advance of their press deadline. Send postcards or call your friends in the area to help stack the deck in your favor. Never rely completely on the bookstore or group's publicity efforts.

It takes lots of teamwork and planning to pull off a successful book signing. Location and timing are important considerations. Does your book have any tie-in to newsworthy events, holidays, or other local happenings? In many locations, a book reading or a free seminar is much more promotable than a book signing. These give a greater opportunity for media exposure on the day before the event and for you to present substantial material that will grab your audience and turn the merely curious into eager buyers.

When a major publisher creates an author tour, it is done along with an aggressive media campaign. And major publishers pick up the tab for book dealers who host big name author signings. So guess what? If you initiate the contact for a book signing, the book dealer (bookstore owner) may expect you to carry the brunt of the expense and the promotional responsibility. The bookstore will probably develop some kind of a promotional piece, but the rest may be up to you. Therefore, you'd better be prepared to be asked to pay for your book signing event. You may be asked to pay for publicizing your signing, and to pay for your own transportation, meals, and motel, if necessary. It is not uncommon for these signings to end up very small where only a couple dozen copies are sold. Autograph parties enable you to make friends, but don't look for a big return in sales. Don't be disappointed, just expect it. The nature of the beast is that normal signings average ten, twenty, sometimes thirty books. Rare indeed are the big occasions where an author is selling hundreds or thousands. These are for the hottest big name authors and best-selling books.

When you're realistic about book signings, you'll view each as a building block in your successful marketing structure. Any book signing serves as a great distribution function. Ultimately, distribution is the most crucial element to the success of a book. It's always wise economically to arrange as many book signings as you can where you travel to by car. That way if you don't get the media attention to draw a big crowd, you will not be out mega bucks in travel and lodging expense.

But there are some pro-active steps you can take to up the ante towards success:

1. Targeted mailings with follow-up phone calls and e-mails are essential to ensuring a well-attended event.

2. Double-check with the store manager several times before your scheduled event to see how publicity, excitement, and pre-sales are going. Design a flier (bag stuffer) announcing the upcoming signing and send them to the bookstore manager. Have the store clerks insert the fliers into each purchase bag for at least two full weeks and weekends in advance of your signing.

3. Create some bright, eye-catching posters featuring a copy of your book cover and announcing the date and time of your signing. Encourage the store manager to display them in several prominent places: front window, near cash register, community bulletin board near the lounge.

4. Get the local paper to do an author interview and/or book review scheduled to come out the week before your in-store appearance. Make sure the area papers receive your interesting press release announcing your reading and/or signing. Check early with your newspaper for specifics on deadline, editor to submit to, and any publication requirements.

5. Even higher foot traffic is guaranteed when you can get a local radio interview or talk show date. If you can't secure the interview, then at least make sure an announcement is made on the community events calendar the week prior to your event. Deadlines for turning

in these announcements are normally at least two weeks prior to the event, and sometimes even sooner. Call the station and secure length and submission requirements.

Theresa Walsh, print promotions director for the B&B Media Group, suggests that to get the word out, retailers should "promote the event through bag stuffers, endcaps, church fliers, community bulletin boards, postcard mailers, 'autograph' stickers and other promotional pieces" ("Author Tours: Boom or Bust?" by G. Sean Fowlds, *Christian Retailing,* March 18, 1999).

Remember, the more media attention you attract, the better the odds that you won't be embarrassed or bored at your book signing. Bookstore managers are not publicists and often do not have either the time or ability to help create the publicity splash that you need. Go the extra mile to help insure a quality event, and then pray a lot and leave it all in God's hands.

As an author, you must be prepared to do your part in personal interaction with the customers during the event. Depending upon the store and the situation, you may be expected to not only do a signing, but also give a reading or speaking presentation. Donna Dightman Baker of Dightman's Bible Book Center in Tacoma, Washington, told *Christian Retailing* (March 18, 1999), "It's also helpful if the author comes prepared to mix and mingle with the people, otherwise there's no ministry, and people go away disappointed."

Experienced authors of many book signings recommend that authors can be better prepared for their moment in the spotlight by taking along an autograph party kit containing things you might need in a pinch: sharpie extra-fine point marker pens (or your personal favorite signing pen), business cards, scissors, thumbtacks, scotch tape, press releases, fliers, Kleenex, cough drops, water bottle, 3" x 5" cards, bowl of peppermints or Hershey kisses, enlarged book cover posters, bookmarks, postcards, and a wire or plastic book stand that will fit your featured book.

Simply being a good author doesn't make you a good people person, so always go prayed up, rested up, and gregarious. Most people don't care as much about obtaining an autograph as they do about gaining insight into the author whose books they are reading. Any little extra down home touches or information you can provide for guests at the signing can change this rather generic book party into a major event and happening.

Immediately after a bookstore event, be sure to send the store owner and store manager a thank-you note for their helpful support of your new book.

What Trade Shows, Community Fairs, Regional Gatherings Are Appropriate for Promotion of Your Book?

Exhibiting your book at festivals and conventions can be a fun way to get your book viewed by lots of potential buyers. Consider sharing booth costs with other self-publishers or with your small press distributor. This can be a fairly inexpensive way to become better known in your own city and county and state.

Statistics tell us that less than 50 percent of all book sales actually occur in a bookstore. What other types of businesses or locations would work well for your particular book title? To get into these markets, you are going to have to put on your salesman's hat and do a lot of leg work, but it may well be worth your efforts.

There will be other conventions, like the ABA or CBA, Denominational Conventions, and Association Conferences, where you will not have the opportunity to display and sell your book—they are simply too costly for you to exhibit in. But there's nothing to stop you from doing a lot of networking with bookstore owners and managers as you wait in lines and rub elbows in the aisles, hallways, and coffee shops. Always carry one copy of your book and a huge stack of brochures, business cards, and bookmarks in your briefcase or tote bag. Don't be shy. After all, the reason they are there is to buy books. Book shows are fun and a source of constant learning about the book trade.

Local country fairs, homeschool conventions, Christian Education Conferences, arts and crafts shows, and community book fairs and festivals all offer an opportunity for exposure to a lot of people. You'll want to get creative or enlist the help of an artistic/creative friend to come up with an attractive display and booth design. But once you have a theme and build/paint shelves, racks, signs, and eye-catching attention-getters, all you have to do is appear and meet and greet the passersby. All of these opportunities provide name recognition, instant cash, and the opportunity to gather hundreds of names for your direct mail lists. By offering free drawings for your book if they'll fill out a ticket or leave their business card for the draw, you'll have instant addresses and potential buyers for your next mailing blitz. These gatherings also give you the opportunity to do some old-fashioned bartering or exchanging your book for another exhibitor's book (or art or craft). It's one more way to promote goodwill and possibly earn future sales. Of course, you'll stick in a brochure or business card with every book you give away in this manner.

Essence Publishing gained exposure for its books by taking authors Esther Peters Balisky (*In Grandpa's Shoes*) and Robert Sandberg (*To Tame a Savage Heart*) to the 1999 Christian Workers Conference in Spokane, Washington.

If you cannot afford to rent a booth on your own, then look around and find other authors with similar products

ESTHER PETERS BALISKY

In Grandpa's Shoes portrays one of many Reformation Christian families who fled persecution as they immigrated from Holland to Prussia to Russia and finally to the United States and Canada. The suffering they endured to preserve the faith of their fathers is a dominant theme. (Available from Essence, 1998, $24.95, plus $3 shipping.) Esther says, "In the summer of 1999 we took a ministry trip across Canada. At PRBI College, I gave seminars on 'How to Write Your Life Story' to complement my book, *In Grandpa's Shoes*. The seminars went so well that the first day people were turned away from the door. *In Grandpa's Shoes* are in bookstores in Kansas, Canada, Seattle, and in numerous libraries and churches."

ROBERT SANDBERG

To Tame a Savage Heart is a true story of missionary adventure—a story of jungle treks, death threats, snakes, and many miracles. Robert and his wife, Ruth, were the first Wycliffe Bible Translators to the Secoya and Orejon Indian tribes of the Amazon jungle. They served in Peru, South America, for eight and a half years. (Available from Essence, 1999, $14.95, plus $3 shipping.)

that would be a good match. Homeschool conventions have become a particularly popular location for self-published authors to gain wide exposure and sell a lot of books. Small press publisher Penny Lent (*Young Writer's Market Manual* and *Young Writer's Manuscript Manual*, Kaleidoscope Press) has teamed up with best-selling author Colleen Reece (Barbour Inspirational Romances and *Writing Smarter Not Harder ... The Workbook Way*, Kaleidoscope Press) and several other authors to rent booth space at the Washington Homeschool Organization (WHO) annual convention in June at the Western Washington Fairgrounds in Puyallup. "Be careful that you don't put more authors together in a booth than it will comfortably handle. And don't plan to stock a whole bunch of other author's materials, unless they are going to be there to sell their own stuff," suggests Colleen. Typically at these conventions there will be a lot of autograph seekers. You do not have time to sell your stuff, talk to customers, autograph books, and be watching the entire booth and someone else's wares. It takes a complete team effort for the entire exhibit time, and it takes a large enough booth for the four to six authors that are going to share the rent.

PAT PFEIFFER

At the Spokane Christian Workers Conference, self-published author Pat Pfeiffer has for many years had a booth "Writers Helping Writers" that attracts hundreds of wanna-be writers by offering free advice and a free manuscript critique service. Besides selling an array of Writer's Digest resource books, Pat has found this a great way to get exposure for her historical novel, *Above All Women ... The Story of the Virgin Mary*. About her book Pat says, "I spent ten years studying Mary's life and discovered some amazing things." *Small Press* magazine review said Pat's book "is a down-to-earth portrayal which attempts to present Mary as a real person of great vulnerability, humanity and faith. While there is admittedly limited scriptural reference to Mary, author Patricia Pfeiffer has relied on general historical research, common sense and imagination to fill in the blanks, to recreate Mary's world and life events from her childhood to her death which Pfeiffer places during Herod Agrippa's relentless purge of Christians from his political landscape."

To get even more attention at a convention, she recommends that you offer to teach a workshop. Pat has taught several through the years. In 2000, her topic is: "Writing For Take-Home Papers." A sure way to get published. Write stories, articles, etc. for Sunday School papers for ages four to twelve. (Pat's book is available from the author. Write: The Parchments, Box 104, Otis Orchards WA 99027. $14.95, plus $3 shipping.)

FIVE

Who'll Be Your Biggest Allies?

Securing Book Reviews

Here it pays to run headlong into the game of securing book reviews, but know that realistically it is a big gamble. With more than 150,000 new books being produced every year, the statistics show that only one in ten ever get reviewed, especially by one of the mega-reviewers (and *Publisher's Weekly* and *The New York Times* rarely review self-published books).

But there are still plenty of periodicals and newspapers that will review your book *if* they or their readers have special interest in your topic. It's well worth your time and effort to find the publications who would have an editorial interest in your book topic. Don't overlook the editors and columnists who cover your topic in any kind of magazine or newspaper. Even a mention (if not a review) in one of these columns can create interest. Finding publication "matches" increases your ability to secure reviews which may be rewarded by a significant increase in sales.

Plan to give away a generous number of review copies. The results may give your book a healthy sales life. This is where the quality of the book editing will pay off. If a reviewer feels there is literary merit to what they are reading, you are more likely to get consideration and high marks than if your book comes off as poorly focused, sloppily edited, and written by an amateur.

Another tactic you'd be wise to try is to call all of your writer friends, freelance book reviewers, and respected authorities on your topic who would be especially receptive to your book, and ask if they'd be willing to write a review and submit it to the particular publications they have an "in" with. Whichever method you choose, always contact the publication for specific guidelines and advice before mailing review copies.

When trying for your share of the library market—church, public, or school—remember that a book with a spine is almost mandatory for shelving and cataloguing. Spiral bindings can become the kiss of death for ever getting a book into a library system.

Book Reviewers

Catholic Library World
Mary E. Gallagher, editorial chairman
291 Springfield St.
Chicopee MA 01013-2839
(413) 594-2761; FAX: (413) 594-7418
gallagherm@elms.edu; http://www.cathla.org

Book and video reviews 300-500 words. Reviewers cover areas such as theology, spirituality, pastoral, professional, juvenile books and material.

CBA Marketplace
Monique Bos, Book Editor
PO Box 200
Colorado Springs CO 80901
(719) 576-7880; FAX: (719) 576-0795
publications@cbaonline.org; www.cbaonline.org
Galleys for review should be submitted three months before publication date. Submit with title, author, publisher, binding, ISBN, and price information. *CBA Marketplace* will request cover art and a galley replacement if the book is selected for review. Book reviews are 100-150 words.

Christian Library Journal
Nancy Hesch, Editor/Publisher
671 Sheri Ln.
Sheridan WY 82801-5430
nancyhclj@aol.com
Book and video reviews 200-400 words.

Christian Retailing
Sean Fowlds, Book Editor
600 Rinehart Rd.
Lake Mary FL 32746
(407) 333-0600; FAX: (407) 333-7133

Church & Synagogue Libraries
Judith Janzen, Executive Director
PO Box 19357
Portland OR 97280-0357

(503) 244-6919; FAX: (503) 977-3734
csla@worldaccessnet.com
http://www.worldaccessnet.com/~csla.
Book and video reviews one to two paragraphs.

Church Libraries
Lin Johnson, Editor
9731 N. Fox Glen Dr. #6F
Niles IL 60714-5861
(847) 296-3964; FAX: (847) 296-0754
linjohnson@compuserve.com
http://members.aol.com/ECLAssoc/index.html
Book, music, video, and cassette reviews by assignment
75-150 words. Requires disk or e-mail submission copied
into message.

NRB (National Religious Broadcasters)
Christine L. Pryor, Editor
7839 Ashton Ave.
Manassas VA 20109
(703) 330-7000; FAX: (703) 330-6996
cpryor@nrb.com; www.nrb.org

Publishers Weekly
245 W 17th St
New York NY 10011
(212) 463-6758; FAX: (212) 463-6631
www.publishersweekly.com
Galleys submitted for review should reach Forecasts at
least three months prior to the month of publication. Each
galley should specify: title, author, illustrator, pub. date,
price, ISBN, number of pages & illustrations, first printing,
ad/promo budget, if noteworthy, and rights information, if

applicable. Galleys for adult religion books should be sent to Jana Riess (3535 Waterworks Road, Winchester, KY 40391; 606-744-5558); for children's religion, send galleys to Elizabeth Devereaux at PW's mailing address. All other galleys should go to PW's mailing address.

In Sally Stuart's *Christian Writers' Market Guide* (published annually by Harold Shaw/Waterbrook), there is a long list of 184 religious publications that say they publish book reviews. The list includes publications in the categories of: adult/general, children, Christian education/library, missions, music, pastors/leaders, teen/young adult, women, writers.

A media list can run into thousands of contact names. If you are economizing, you will have to be wise in picking your targets. Most will not announce a book simply because you send them a press release announcement and/or sample review. They want to see the book for themselves. Publications that specialize in the area of your book topic should also be on this list. Don't overlook your denomination's periodicals and newsletters, as well as church newsletter and local community newspapers.

Radio and Television Interviews

How do you get those coveted radio and television interviews? Ask! If you are not going to hire a publicist who will make all of the contacts for you, then you're going to have to do it yourself. It will take a lot of phone calls and a lot of follow-up to connect with the right program hosts, but there is no substitute for persistence. This is the time to put on your professional PR hat and go for it. Professionalism, persistence, and politeness are your three keys to successfully open very important doors.

> *Professionalism, persistence, and politeness are your three keys to successfully open very important doors.*

Before you make those calls, you must know the programs you're approaching and understand their audience. For a *Directory of Religious Media,* listing all the Christian radio stations, radio programs, television stations, television programs, radio producers, periodicals, book publishers, agencies and services, and more, contact National Religious Broadcasters at (703) 330-7000 ext. 516 or the NRB store at www.nrb.org/store.htm. Features include 4,700 plus listings, key personnel, e-mail and Web sites. Cost: $79.95 for non-members, plus $4 shipping. It is also available on CD-Rom for $295. Another valuable resource is *How to Sell Your Book ... Through Easily Booked Christian Radio Interview Shows* (see Bibliography in Chapter 10).

Most producers will not book a guest just because that person has written a book. The potential interviewee must have more going than that—an interesting subject, a "hot" issue, an unusual slant. Therefore, it's important that the data you submit when you send your book includes topics you'd like to talk about. Program producers are interested in one thing: How will this benefit or be of interest to our listeners or viewers? Make sure you have ideas for "themes" for their show. This allows you to give a well-thought-out, to-the-point presentation, and will make you more than just another pushy author. Think stories. Everyone loves a good storyteller, and this is what a radio talk show host and producer will remember about you. Also, let them know that you have a complete media kit with potential interview questions ready to send them in advance of the program.

If you make a cold call at an inconvenient time to the program host you need to talk to, then ask when a more appropriate time to call would be. One television public affairs director offers this advice: "Producers receive many letters and calls daily. It's not always easy to remember every contact. So when you make your follow-up call, it is important to give your name, title, organization, and the reason you're calling."

BEING YOUR OWN PUBLICIST

- Pray—a lot!
- Pitch letter—grab attention!
- Press kit—the sell job
- Phone call—follow up.

If you're prepared for future interviews, you can also help prepare your interviewers. Fact sheets, synopsis, press release, and list of suitable discussion questions can all play a part in guaranteeing that the person interviewing you will be better prepared to ask pertinent questions. It is the rare interviewer that has actually had the time to read your book in advance. This is your opportunity to help him understand your topic and your focus. Always you'll want to stress the benefits that your book offers the reader. But beware—there is no guarantee that you will be asked any question off your prepared list. When you agree to go on a radio or TV show, you have basically told them, "Ask me anything."

Radio interviewers are usually looking for people with how-to books. They have a lot of time to fill and they want an author who knows their subject, understands what interests other people, and can teach listeners something in an entertaining way. If your subject is controversial, that's all the better for some of today's talk show hosts. But you'd better be able to intelligently stand up for your opinion.

Be interesting, informative, and funny—these are key ingredients for keeping an audience's attention, and for being invited back to appear with your local radio and television hosts. Remember, if you are talking on the radio, this automatically makes you the expert. Tell the truth and don't be boring about it. Establish a "point of connection" with your listener. Each listener wants to feel that you are talking to him personally. Get to the point. Remember that the point of your appearance is to provide information and to help the audience, not to simply "hawk" your book. If you do a good job, the book sales will naturally follow.

> *Remember, if you are talking on the radio, this automatically makes you the expert.*

Be pointed, specific, and concrete in your answers and never succumb to rambling. Work in the title of your book and where it can be purchased at every opportunity, but don't be obnoxious about it. You don't want the interview to sound like one long commercial. You need to be conscientious about answering the questions you are asked. Remember, don't give away the whole book. You are merely trying to tweak interest so people will rush out and buy it. They won't need to if you have already given away all your trade secrets.

It is not unusual these days to do multiple phone interviews from the comfort of your home. These talk shows can last for as much as an hour or more and provide wonderful exposure for your book. You'll feel less caged in and more relaxed during your phone interviews if you use a phone with a 25-foot cord.

Many headset phones are on the market today, which give you the extra ability to keep both of your hands free for note taking or leafing through book pages. The extra freedom to stand up and walk around will help you gain both energy and confidence. When doing your interview by phone, you'll want to: make sure you won't be interrupted; prepare a cheat sheet of important points you want to make; know the producer, host, station call letters, and phone number of the program conducting the interview.

Keep a well-marked copy of your book within arms reach during all interviews. Paper clip, sticky note tab, or highlight the pages that are particularly important for their statistics or quotes. It is imperative that you are able to find these "clinchers" at a moment's notice. One more important tip for doing phone interviews from home: Make sure your call waiting is turned off. Nothing is more annoying than to have that inevitable click go across the air. Also, keep a glass of water near by for the inevitable dry mouth syndrome of speakers or a sudden coughing spell.

If making a television appearance, remember the professional's rules: wear comfortable clothing, solid colors (not white) and not busy prints, and no jangling jewelry. Do not talk with your hands, it's too distracting. Get the make-up department to touch up your face. Talk to the interviewer and not the TV camera. Answer the interviewer's questions fully, but don't go on so long that it sounds like a monologue. Remember that you will have to be extremely focused about the message of your book. You normally have about a seven-minute discussion with the talk show host to squeeze in the message of your 300-page book. Always use your natural speaking voice. Make sure you take a clean copy of your book to be able to show the viewing audience. Practice and try to polish your performance before ever stepping in front of the camera. When the program starts and you are introduced, you should concentrate on being real, polite, honest, informative, enthusiastic, and mostly concerned about lifting up Jesus. There is a delicate, desired balance of being spontaneous yet not overrunning the host.

Avail yourself of the opportunity to give your toll-free (or your distributor's) ordering number several times during your interview. When doing in-person radio or TV interviews, be sure to write down the address or toll-free number where people can call or write to order books directly from you—or from your distributor/wholesaler depending on what method of fulfillment you have selected. The order information should be left with the switchboard operator and the program office.

Authors who give the best interviews display confidence, have verbal energy, seem comfortable in a one-on-one situation, and are not intimidated by the studio or the host. One of the best traits for television appearances is genuineness; a viewing audience can spot a phony showman or an expert in an instant.

After the taping or broadcast, always study the videotape critically. Look for your speech patterns, gestures, posture, unpleasant habits, content, anecdotes, and mistakes. This post-show analysis can mean the difference between one-timers and regulars on the talk-show circuit. The successful interviewee will always concentrate on improving and becoming more powerful.

You're not through until the follow-up is done: Always send thank-you notes. These follow-up letters are a means for keeping in touch and an encouraging reminder that you'd welcome a call back. Basically you're saying, "I was really happy to do your show. It was a pleasure to work with you and I felt that it went really well. I'd welcome the opportunity to do another broadcast."

One radio or television interview may help get the buzz going and can begin a spiral of attention, but God is the only one who can sustain the success.

Is the payoff worth the effort? Most authors would give you a resounding "yes!" The radio and TV programs will increase your offer of speaking engagements, presentations at conferences, workshops, and churches. All of these speaking opportunities allow you a place to both spread your message and sell your books.

Other Authors/Speakers/Organizations

Books that receive the "seal of approval" from other authors/speakers, groups, and associations tend to sell in greater quantities than books fighting the "unknown" factor. When you offer your book at a bulk sales rate for other speakers to sell, or for an organization to use in their fund-raising campaigns, this increases the opportunity for word-of-mouth sales to kick in.

MARVIN MICHAEL

Marvin first self-published *A Passion For Flying ... Exciting Stories of a Boeing Test Pilot* in 1996. His back cover copy contains a fast-paced summary, high-powered endorsements, and an impressive author bio—all sure ingredients to promote sales.

"See Michael and crew parachuting out of a wildly oscillating B-17 Flying Fortress. Sit in the cockpit of his huge B-29 Superfortress Receiver braving enormous hazards as he delicately maneuvers within 25 feet of the tanker to take on fuel through the highly acclaimed Boeing boom inflight refueling system. Experience his adventures flying a 36-year-old DC-3 in famine relief in Ethiopia. Read his exciting stories during 60 years of flying."

Because of Marvin's association with the Boeing Museum of Flight in Seattle, his book has sold extremely well in the museum gift shop. Marvin earned the Silver C soaring badge and his picture hangs as a Hall of Fame member of the OX5 Aviation Pioneers. He flew an airplane as a pilot-in-command after his 80th birthday, becoming a member of the United Flying Octogenarians.

His book outlining his achievements contributed to his being inducted into the Pathfinder Hall of Fame on November 6, 1999, for his pioneering contributions to the development of aviation in the Northwest. The Museum of Flight and the Pacific Northwest Section of the American Institute of Aeronautics and Astronautics presented the prestigious award at the Eighteenth Annual Pathfinders Awards Banquet, a black-tie, white silk flying scarf event held at the Seattle Museum of Flight.

Because of continuous professional promotion by Marvin, and the rapid sales and high demand all the attention has generated, *A Passion for Flying* was picked up by CBA publisher Ambassador-Emerald International of South Carolina and Northern Ireland, and released in their new edition in December 1999. *A Passion for Flying* is available from the author: Marvin Michael, 9101-48 Steilacoom Rd. SE, Olympia WA 98513. Send $11.95, plus $3 shipping.

Mom/Family/Friends/Church

In your push for attention, don't ignore those who know you best and who may become your biggest cheerleaders. Statistics tell us that each of your satisfied customers will tell at least five more people. Load these people up with bookmarks, postcards, brochures, whatever they need to help you spread the word.

Send notes, press clippings, or even a newsletter to make your friends, family, and associates feel like insiders, and to keep them enthused about helping you achieve your mission. Show your thanks to all who have helped you on your journey.

Team with family and friends to hold a big launch party to kick off your book publication. Launch parties have been held successfully at homes, museums, art galleries, churches, halls, historical mansions, lighthouses, ferries. Make it festive, unusual, and memorable.

SIX

How to Keep Your Sanity and Not a Warehouse Full of Books

Develop a Strategic Sales Plan—It Pays to Go After Sales Outside of the Bookstore

Timely events—tying your book to calendar events—always gives you a chance at free publicity.

Look into the possibility of putting up displays in related places—churches, camps, gift shops, hospitals, doctor's offices, etc.

Exhibit and/or teach seminars at specialized audience conventions and workshops—Homeschool Conventions, Christian Education Conventions, Missions Conferences, etc.

Write a lot of articles. The more articles you can generate from your book's topic, the greater your chance of placing them with important and widely-circulated periodicals. When you know your target audience and what magazines they read, it isn't too difficult to study the guidelines and prepare articles specifically that meet your reader's need.

Plan Ahead for Needed $$, But Don't Mortgage the House

Every book publisher, whether a large house or a one-title self-publisher, plans a marketing budget based on projected sales. Before you start writing the checks, estimate the amount of money you will need for promotional expenses. This can range from just a couple hundred dollars for fliers and postcards, to thousands of dollars for a comprehensive plan that includes mailings, ads, and tours.

Income from sales of books seems to just trickle in. From wholesalers, distributors, consignment bookstores, etc., it could take thirty to ninety days before you see any money. Don't count on fast money. Have plenty of cash on hand to keep you producing and shipping out books and PR materials until you start to generate a consistent cash flow.

Invoicing

One of your early decisions will be on printing your invoice. While it is important to have the standard information on your invoice—title of book, list price, discount, net amount, and postage/shipping costs—it is also very smart to indicate that prepayment is required. While getting as many orders as possible prepaid, there will be times when you are going to have to invoice your customer. Invoicing of customers should be allowed: (1) when the customer is a friend or relative, and you are reasonably sure they will pay right away; (2) you are putting your books on consignment at a writers conference, retreat, or similar function where you know they will be settling up with payment after the event ends.

When shipping multiple books to bookstores, churches, or other organizations, always keep a copy of the original purchase order. This becomes your proof of order and shipment should you have trouble collecting. Filing invoices and keeping up with collections are essential. You can't afford to become the First National Bank for deadbeat customers. Always make complete memos (including name of person ordering) when orders are phoned in. These could become records that you will have to produce for the IRS or others.

There is no special postal book rate in Canada. So be sure to adjust your retail price to allow for the expensive mailing costs.

Keeping a list of everyone that requests, reviews, and buys your book is essential for follow-up PR. In publicity and promotion you have to be thinking down the road—not only about the first hot-off-the-press year. Carefully look at all direct mailings you do for their cost versus effectiveness at securing orders. If you do not recoup two and a half times your costs of printing and mailing, then you may need to reconsider. Things to consider include: a bulk mailing permit, and the best months to do direct mailing.

ORDER FORM/INVOICE

Writers Information Network
PO Box 11337
Bainbridge Island WA 98110
Tel: (206) 842-9103
Fax: (206) 842-0536

Date:_____

Sold to: _____
Ship to: _____
Buyer: _____
Terms/Special Instructions: _____
When Shipped: _____
How Shipped: _____
Salesperson: _____
Buyer's Signature: _____

Quantity	ISBN	Title/Description	Unit Price	Total

Shipping ($3.00 first book, $1.00 each add. book): _____

Prepaid, COD Orders and Credit Card Payment
2% off (Call for Approval)   _____

❑ Mastercard   ❑ Visa

Credit Card #: _____ Exp.: _____
Signature: _____

Sales Tax

If you're going to sell books, you may need to collect tax and turn it over to the state, depending on your volume of business. Check with your state tax authorities for details. If applicable, the first step is to obtain your resale (or seller's) permit. You must collect sales tax when you make retail sales in your own state. However, sales tax is not charged when your book is purchased by a bookstore or distributor who will then resell the book. You also will not charge sales tax when the book is sold out-of-state.

Income Tax

Because you are the sole proprietor of your business, you are responsible for reporting income received from book sales and may be liable for income taxes. Calculate the net earnings of your business on a Schedule C of the 1040 Form. The profit of your business as calculated on Schedule C is then reported as income. The good news is that you can deduct all of your business costs from your gross income, and then you just have to report what's left as personal income. Save all those postage, printing, copying, gas, and other receipts that are necessary in running your business. Check with your local tax accountant or income tax authorities to ensure you meet all reporting requirements.

DID YOU KNOW—ARE YOU DOING IT?

- As a self-employed writer, you must use Form 1040 in filing your taxes along with Schedule C—Profit or Loss from Business.

- As a self-employed writer, you must also file a Schedule

SE (Self-Employment Tax) if you have a net income of over $433 in a single year.

- There are many rules for claiming a home office deduction, including: It must be a distinct space specifically used for business and nothing else. It must be the primary location of your income-producing activity. Over 50 percent of your income-generating activity must happen in this office.

- You can deduct 50 percent of any meal where you discuss your business of writing, even if that person is a friend.

- Business-related travel is deductible. Trips to writers conferences, research for a book or article, travel for interviews, etc. are part of furthering the writer's career. However, certain criteria must be met, and sometimes the travel expenses must be prorated between business and non-business activities.

- The cost of advertising for your business is deductible.

- Fees for tax advice related to your writing business and for preparation of the tax forms related to your business are deductible.

- Consumable office supplies for your writing business are deductible and can be listed either under Office Expense or Supplies.

- Magazine and newspaper subscriptions, as well as books, videos, and software may all be deducted—even if they're not specifically related to your market—if these materials enhance your creative process. Membership to writing organizations may also be deducted under Other Expenses.

- The cost of writers conventions, conferences, university classes on journalism, seminars on grammar usage, and correspondence courses on writing are all allowable deductions for a writing business.

- Get a receipt for everything, even if you pay by check. The IRS doesn't consider a canceled check to be sufficient proof of most purchases.

- Take the word "miscellaneous" out of your vocabulary. Find a general category, which you list under "Other" on Schedule C. Self-published author and tax consultant Sandy Cathcart says, "If you are truly operating your writing activities as a business and are keeping careful and complete records, you should not fear an IRS audit. It is simply a matter of producing your records and answering their questions."

Sandy is a writer and a licensed tax preparer with the state of Oregon. Used by permission from Totally Honest Tax Tips for Writers. *Detailed instructions and charts in a 32-page, 8 1/2" x 11" spiral-bound book. Send $10 (covers shipping) check to Sandy Cathcart, 341 Flounce Rock Road, Prospect, OR 97536. 75222.3643@compuserve.com.*

JOHN VONHOF

My book, *Fixing Your Feet ... Preventive Maintenance and Treatments for Foot Problems of Runners, Hikers, and Adventure Racers,* is written for athletes who stress their feet beyond what any normal person would imagine. As a self-published book, it has great potential, when they know about it. By subscribing to sport specific Internet e-mail lists, I gain exposure to thousands of potential readers. For *Fixing Your Feet*, I am on three lists and any time I see an e-mail that asks a question about foot care, I respond. All my e-mails have my "signature" with my book title and web site address. Interested readers can click on my web site link and go directly to an order form. Yes, there is a time trade-off—reviewing e-mails and answering foot related questions does take time, but it has given me great credibility and exposure. Any writer who self-publishes should investigate the large number of e-mail lists on the Internet. Generally, there are no costs to subscribe to these lists. Each list has guidelines and a list owner/moderator. While they may have restrictions on your advertising your book directly to the list, they allow most discussion topics related to the list subject. Start at www.liszt.com, the mailing list directory. When you find a list related to the subject of your book, subscribe to it and send an e-mail to the list introducing yourself. Customize your e-mail signature with your name, e-mail, book title, and web site. Then monitor the list for related questions, answer them, and establish yourself as an authority and an author. You will sell books and make a lot of friends!

John Vonhof, Fixing Your Feet ... Preventive Maintenance and Treatments for Foot Problems of Runners, Hikers, and Adventure Racers *($14.95, plus $3 shipping), available at: http://www.footworkpub.com/feet.*

SEVEN

Establishing a Successful Web Site

Contributed by Ernst S. Sibberson

The Internet has brought a new dimension to the ability of authors to obtain free publicity. Besides sending e-mail messages to all your family, friends, and associates, the endless possibilities include: putting announcements about your book on bulletin boards, in chat rooms, and on your own web pages.

Establishing Your Web Site

Marketing yourself online has become such a popular enterprise that dozens of books have been written about it, courses are being offered in businesses and community colleges, and online consultants are setting up to help you in your business. We will only mention the tip of the iceberg as it relates to the author—in making you aware of the endless possibilities this new technology offers you.

Whether or not a Web site will result in lots of sales for your book, there are some definite benefits. It pays to get online and communicate with people in your area of specialization and with other writers and authors. You will gain professional knowledge, and you never know when you will capture referrals, speaking engagements, and sales.

There's no doubt about it: Web surfers are a restless lot. If you are going to capture attention, your site must have a clear focus and interest-holding value. Lots of Web page software is now available to make the work of getting your site up a lot less technical. Some authors have gone so far as to put their "press kit" on their Web site. The assembled contents include everything a media person would need to write about the book or interview the author—a fact sheet, author bio, quotes from celebrities or well-known authors/personalities, table of contents, chapter excerpts, interview questions, and down-loadable pictures of the book cover and the author.

The clutter of the Internet and the sheer vastness of it makes it both baffling and challenging. Yes, you will do all the right things by getting listed with search engines and directories, but don't neglect including your Web site and your e-mail address in your traditional ads, publicity pieces, and printed materials (brochures, business cards, and letterhead).

Clean organization with bite-size chunks of information and easily definable purpose are the hallmarks of a good Web page. Restrict yourself to a limited number of concepts or thoughts per page, but keep the Web surfer interested enough to click the buttons to other pages on your site for intriguing tidbits of information.

Your Basic Web Page

- *Meta Tags*

Meta tags are unseen codes hidden beneath your web page. These "tags" are a very important part of your web page—helping search engines index your page content. There are three basic meta tags you need to be concerned with to ensure search engine recognition: Page Title, Page Description, and Keywords.

TITLE: Your page title appears on the web search engines when your page is found. Every page on your Web site should have a proper title. This includes your company and/or product name and a brief description of the product or page content. Use descriptive key words in such a manner as to "sell the sizzle, not the steak." A title is between five and eight words. Remove as many "filler" words as possible from the title, such as "the," "and," etc.

DESCRIPTION: The description is an extension of the title. It is a summary of key points important to the content of your Web page. They should match words that someone would enter in a search to find your Web page, product, or product category. Select the most important twenty key-words, and write a careful 200 to 250 character (including spaces) sentence or two. There is no need to repeat any word used in the page title. Keep your description readable but tight. Again, eliminate as many "filler" or "throwaway" words as you can (such as: and, the, a, an, company, etc.) to make room for the important words—the keywords which do the actual work for you.

KEYWORDS: Keywords tell search engines what categories you would like to be listed under. They alone will not make a significant difference in your search engine position. However, used wisely, they will help you connect with the thoughts of your online surfer.

For example, your book is about troubled teens. Some good meta tags would be: *youth, teens, coping, high school, children, K12, bullies, grade school, neighborhood, peer pressure, troubled, enemies, friends, parents, bullying, divorce, parenting, kids, nasty, mean, neighbors, etc.* Do some brainstorming to come up with additional keywords. Do not repeat the same word more than three to six times. Try to use variations of words, phrases, and do not put similar words back-to-back.

Your key words should reflect what you imagine someone might type as a query when searching to find your site. Do not stuff your meta tags with countless or unrelated keywords. This will cause your site to be demoted or banned from most search engines. Limit your keywords to about 870 characters including commas. Keywords should be separated by commas—no spaces are required.

The Web Page

While Web pages can be just about infinite in length, try to limit them to one or two screen lengths. Use plenty of "white space." Be brief in describing your product or information. Make the most of the first twenty-five words of your web page. Detail exactly what the page is about. Use words that specifically describe your product. If further information is required, direct the viewer to additional Web pages for more information. Use words that you have placed in your description and keyword meta tags.

Use graphics sparingly and keep them as small as possible. Graphics greatly affect the "load time" of the viewer's browser. If your page takes longer than five seconds to load, you will probably lose your viewer to another site. Avoid using frames—some search engines will not recognize your page if it has frames. Ease of use is the key determinant when considering how to design your Web page. Is your Web page quick to download? Can visitors find the information they seek in just a few glances or click of the mouse?

Getting It Discovered

You are the needle in the haystack—and that haystack is big! Conservative estimates put the number of Web pages on the Internet at over two billion and growing. Getting discovered takes a lot of work and time. The key to getting discovered is exposure, exposure, exposure. The more Web pages you have, the better chance you have of being discovered.

For example, you are going to market your book. You could have one long Web page with all of your information on it. That's great. But separating the information into a number of different Web pages—book title and description, summary, author bio, table of contents, sample chapter, and order form—gives you six separate Web pages. Your exposure has been increased six-fold. Also, each page must be linked to one another. This allows the viewer to easily go to each page on your Web site.

• Domain Name

One of the wisest decisions you can make to promote your site is to obtain your own domain name—and at $35 a year, it's a bargain. You can purchase a domain that best describes your business. This will often improve your search engine and directory rankings.

Having your own domain name makes your Web site portable. You can move it from hosting service to hosting service if necessary without ever affecting your Web site. However, if you share a domain name and need to change hosting services, you must redo all your search engine positioning work. And, the benefits of all your other marketing efforts that pointed to the old domain name are then lost.

• Search Engines and Directories

Each individual page of your Web site must be submitted to search engines and directories. The top ranking search engines are: Go.com (same as Infoseek), Excite.com, Lycos.com, Snap.com, AltaVista.com, and Hotbot.com.

This can be a formidable but necessary task. However, there are services on the Internet that will automatically submit your Web pages for you. Some of these are Scrub the Web (http://www.scrubtheweb.com/abs/promo.html) and Submit Express (http://www.submitexpress.com).

Next, submit your Web pages to Yahoo. This is the most important listing of all. Technically, Yahoo is a directory rather than a search engine. Each submission is manually inserted, and sometimes they will edit your description. Be very careful when submitting, and follow their instructions (http://dir.yahoo.com/computers_and_internet).

After submitting your Web pages, be patient! Some search engines take weeks or months before they update their catalogs. AltaVista.com seems to be the fastest—usually within two or three days you will see your pages listed.

Once you are indexed, check your site at least once a week. Strange things happen. Pages disappear from catalogs. Links go awry. Watch for trouble and resubmit if you spot problems. Also, resubmit your pages on a regular basis—

perhaps once a month. *Always* resubmit when you change any information on the page.

Promoting Your Web Site

There are many ways to promote your Web site—both free and fee-based. Seek out as many free methods as you can.

• Swap reciprocal links

Find complementary Web sites and request a reciprocal link to your site. In the Christian community, I have found many sites that will link to your site. Some of them are:

NAME	URL
Goshen	www.goshen.net
The Best Christian Links	www.tbcl.com
Cybergrace	www.cybergrace.com
777 Net	www.777.net
His Net	www.his-net.com
Cross Daily	www.crossdaily.com
Cross Search	www.crosssearch.com
Christian World Daily	www.themissionary.net

Most of these have small banners that you insert on your Web page. More than two or three can make your web page look cluttered. You might even lose your viewer when he clicks on the banner. To eliminate this hazard, place all banners and links on a separate page and link to that page with a comment such as "Check out my favorite links" somewhere near the bottom of your Web page. You can also join a banner exchange program such as Link Exchange at www.linkexchange.com.

- Capture visitor e-mail addresses and request permission to send updates

Create a viewer response form on your web page. Include a checkbox where the visitor can give you permission to e-mail updates about products or services. Now your e-mails to visitors are not "spam." You're responding to their request for more information. Capture first and last name in separate fields so you can market personally to them. But only ask for the information you need or they won't fill out the form.

- Create a signature at the bottom of your e-mail messages

Most e-mail programs allow you to create a "signature" that appears at the end of each message you send. Limit it to six to eight lines: Company name, address, phone number, URL, e-mail address, and a one-phrase description of your unique business offerings. Look for examples on e-mail messages sent to you.

- Ask visitors to bookmark your site

It seems so simple—and you'll be surprised how many will do it.

- Promote your site in mailing lists and news groups

There are thousands of targeted mailing lists and news groups with very specialized interests. Search DejaNews (http://www.dejanews.com) to find sources appropriate to your interests. Find groups where a dialog is taking place.

Don't use aggressive marketing to plug your product or service. Rather, join discussion in a helpful way and let the "signature" at the end of your e-mail message do your marketing for you. People will gradually get to know and trust you, visit your site, and do business with you.

These are just a few free ways of promoting your Web site. I recommend using as many free methods as possible. If these bring in results, then you may want to consider paid advertising to promote your Web site.

Several creative methods have been thought of to analyze your Web site traffic and track your potential customers: (1) Produce a document on your site that encourages people to answer a few questions about themselves in exchange for a discount price on your book; (2) Use an online survey of five or six questions to determine how closely their reading

ERNST S. SIBBERSON

Ernst S. Sibberson started his writing career as a reporter and editor of his college newspaper. After college, he worked for over 25 years as a technical writer for both small and large corporations. A results-oriented publications professional, Ernst has written technical manuals on everything from acoustics to welding, including a writers style guide for aircraft engine component vendors. Now, Ernst is a freelance technical writer, editor, ghostwriter, and Web site developer. He lives with his wife in Sandusky, Ohio. Visit his Web site at: www.bluejaypub.com. His recently self-published manual, *Creating and Promoting Your Website*, is now available. Send $7.95, plus $3 shipping to: Ernst S. Sibberson, PO Box 522, Sandusky OH 44870.

interests match the theme of your book products; (3) Add a discussion board to your Web site so you can find out what the browsers are saying about the theme or topic of your book.

CARMEN LEAL

One Essence author has used the Web very successfully in her writing/speaking career. Carmen Leal is the author of *Faces of Huntington's* (Essence, 1998, $15.95), a book for and about people with Huntington's Disease, and others who care. The book is a beacon of light in what is often a dark world. 30,000 Americans have this terminal neurological disorder.

She is the co-author with Eva Marie Everson of *Pinches of Salt, Prisms of Light* (Essence, 1999, $14.95), a collection of writings about ordinary people doing extraordinary things. Salt and Light is a concept based on the teaching of Jesus found in Matthew 5, and lets us know about people who are making a difference by showing "goodness" in their world.

Carmen's Web site is being used quite effectively to pre-publication announce her book, *WriterSpeaker.com* (Harold Shaw, 2000). Both book and Web site offer valuable tips that any author/speaker can put into use immediately. Her Web links are a quick, easy way to learn what's out there and how to use the Web to your own advantage.

Carmen's personal Web site with further information about her books, speaking, and singing can be accessed at http://www.writerspeaker.com.

EIGHT

Become a Groupie—Go Where the People Are

This is the time to become a joiner and make lots of new acquaintances. Whether it's clubs, associations, writers groups, organizations, Bible studies, or whatever, most have journals, reference books, newsletters, magazines, trade shows, etc. where they are more than eager to list the accomplishments of their members. Many groups are frequently looking for speakers, table talks, and workshop leaders. If your book is inspirational, entertaining, or how-to, you might be the perfect person to fill one of these slots. And all of this adds up to a lot of free publicity.

Judith Appelbaum and Florence Janovic, in their valuable *Writer's Workbook,* remind us that, "Any place people in your target audience gather is a place you might display and/or sell your book." They go on to recommend that you "make up a list of meetings where your book might sell" and then explore the possibility of taking/shipping books and/or order forms to the meetings.

Know Your Reader—Well

Dale Carnegie, author of *How to Win Friends and Influence People,* once said, "You can make more friends in two months by becoming interested in other people than you can in two years by trying to get other people interested in you." As you participate in groups and organizations, leave a trail of good feelings. Be careful not to burn any bridges.

Make the Most of Word-of-Mouth Marketing

What is it? Word-of-mouth marketing is nothing more than one person talking to another person about your book. It often happens by chance without any effort on your part. But other times you can help orchestrate the buzz by making sure that you get positive press from people whose opinions count. So your natural question becomes: "How can I help create the 'word-of-mouth effect' for my book?"

There are no positive, sure-fire ways to get word-of-mouth marketing going, but there are sensible, creative suggestions that can help you.

1. Focus on the service that you are providing your readers. What are you helping them do, learn, accomplish, feel? Whatever you are doing, keep the surprise element, the unexpected in it—that gives people something to talk about.

2. Develop relationships—people love to brag that they know authors by name. Do everything you can to make

your friends and acquaintances feel extra special. Use their names whenever you see them. Send notes or call them just to say how much you appreciate their friendship, support, and business.

3. Try to be thoughtful in your follow-up to special occasions—write thank-you notes. Make book buying and book giving fun, easy, and make your customers comfortable. If your book can be thought of as "comfort food," and if your "do unto others" attitude has won people's confidence in you, then they will love your book and help spread the word.

Network With Key Players: Experts, Authors, Famous People

1. **Keep in touch with your contacts.** If you're a brilliant writer with developing news stories, great book ideas, speaking engagements, etc. but no one knows or is talking about you—it won't help your career. That's where lunches, phone calls, conferences, e-mails, and lots of things have to bite into your writing time. Because they have everything to do with advancing you and your career, they are considered the necessary evil of building your writer's/speaker's reputation and keeping you on people's minds when it comes time to giving out the assignments.

2. **Refine every idea.** "Having a good idea these days is not enough, I'm afraid to say," says a HarperCollins senior editor. Use this three-step approach to make sure your idea is salable: research your subject thoroughly, identify your target market, and keep up with the news so you can tie your book into newsworthy events.

3. **Remember, your calling card is more important than a business card.** Make sure your press release is well-crafted and carefully proofread—it is your calling card—the only way the media will be able to judge you as a writer, a person, and a interview/feature. Give it "plus value." Offer the little extras (photos, sidebars, quotes, endorsements, etc.) that will put you over the top.

4. **Read. Read. Read.** Know where your writing fits into a bookstore's precious shelf space and into the overall trends of the book publishing marketplace. Your best understanding of the marketplace always comes from reading.

5. **What's being done?** You need to be able to explain how your book is different. Knowing your target audience and the competition, and letting potential bookstore buyers know you know, is a sure way to get across the impression that you're a professional.

6. **Use the right pitch.** Every magazine and newspaper section is unique, with their own specific focus, columns, concept of who their readers are, what they want, and how to reach them. Try to get inside the editor's head and determine just who he is appealing to and what the reader expects. Editors need to be shown why your story is ideal for their publication.

7. **Sell yourself.** Your query letter must show an editor/agent why *you* are qualified. Do you have access to sources who are difficult to reach? Do your personal experiences, training, interests, contacts, endorsements, etc. qualify you to write this particular manuscript? Editors are partial to passionate and insightful pieces by writers who have strong connection to their subject matter.

With every query, submit your authors bio, along with (or including) a writing credits list. Editors are asking: "What does the author/writer bring beyond the article/book idea? Who do they know? Who can they quote? Who are their endorsements?

8. **Never lose sight of the fact that there are real people at the other end of the mail.** The more editors and publishers you meet at writers conferences, EPA and CBA conventions, the more people will be anxious to open your envelope when they see your name on the return address.

Keep God in the Equation

Pray a lot. Keep pushing on doors. And be sure you are ready to walk through every door that God opens for you. Ultimately, He's your boss. Most of us write books because we believe that God has given us something to share that will in some way help others. Writing our book is the easy part. Rarely do we stop to think about how much time and energy will be devoted to marketing and selling our book. But this is when we must not get discouraged and give up. When we remain true to God's call and commission, He leads us through all the difficulties and tough stuff to accomplish His purposes. It is good to remember Ephesians 3:20, NKJV: "Now to Him who is able to do exceedingly abundantly above all that we ask or think, according to the power that works in us...."

When it seems that we have come to the end of our road, used up all our ideas and resources, and still have boxes full of books, we need to look up. At the end of ourselves and our self-sufficiency, the God of all creativity is still there waiting for us to rely on Him. Often God wants us to get beyond our pride and conceit and admit our dependence on Him. Sometimes He has to allow us the experience of heartbreak or disappointment so that we will get our priorities straight. This is when we must confess that our feverish plans are to no avail because we never ask God for help. Remember: "God has the power to do all He wills to do. He has both the resources and the ability to work His will in every circumstance" (Ray Pritchard in *Green Pastures, Quiet Waters,* Moody, 1999, p. 52).

NINE

When to Stop Promoting Yourself

When do you get to stop promoting yourself? When you have all the sales, recognition, credibility, and achievement you need or can stand. When you are well-established as a speaker and publisher. When you feel you have moved from the ranks of the "unknown" to the "known" in publishing circles and among bookstore owners.

Very few marketing efforts will give you immediate turnaround. Your promotion efforts will not be instantaneously successful. But keep it going—don't let your marketing efforts take a backseat to everything else you are doing. All PR has a brick wall building effect—layer upon layer upon layer you are getting out there and making yourself and your product known. Each and every effort is a vital complement to all of the other work, speaking, and promoting you have done.

It is a well-known fact that most books have a shelf life—a time of peak sales—of just a couple years. After that you will see your sales figures going downhill. It is up to you to create and maintain a big enough buzz to keep the sales coming in while you still have considerable inventory. Unless you are convinced that you have saturated the market and more advertising or marketing efforts would not pay for themselves in return income, then you'd better keep pushing.

> *Don't give up just before your miracle.*

Don't give up just before your miracle. You must go into this business determined to persevere. It will probably take awhile before you see the results from all of your efforts. There are very few overnight successes in this business. However, if you have a good product you will become recognized—if only you'll persevere. It could take a year or more to get reviewed in the publications that will gain you the most recognition, but it will happen. Persevere!

What you want to keep doing is developing marketing ideas that will enable you to keep generating consumer awareness for your book(s). You can do this by a number of cost-effective ways that will help you gain significant results.

Develop a Marketing Theme

Build all of your advertising efforts around a thematic message. Use concrete words that leave no ambiguity on the part of your readers. Words like "new," "free," "the best," "improved," are all considered power words—use them! Try new formats or unconventional methods for attracting attention to your product. Don't limit your thinking to the traditional methods of print media. Use out of the box ideas to move your marketing efforts to the next level.

Think About Writing Another Book

This is also the time to think about writing and producing another book. Successful self-publishers rarely have only one title. Speakers and teachers maximize their efforts when they have several products they can sell off of their back tables. As a self-publisher, it is better to learn the ropes of the business from your first book, and then go back and publish several others successfully when you are no longer a novice. If you are getting into publishing to produce only one book, unless you feel that book is your heart's passion and a message that must be shared, you'll have to determine if it's worth all your time, money, and efforts.

Self-publishers who end up turning their business into a small press operation estimate that it takes a minimum list of four or five books to get the full benefit of your cost of operation. When you create a line of books, distributors and wholesalers will pay more attention to you. There is not the same risk regarding refunds when one book must be returned, if you can offer credit toward another book from your list. Whether or not you want to have your additional books all written by you, or acquire some by another author, is a point you need to seriously consider. Do you want to be an author or a publisher? It is hard to be working on another book when you know you should be writing news releases, setting up interviews, and hitting the road for sales.

Create a Newsletter

Authors frequently develop a fan club following who want to be informed of new developments in the field of your book: your speaking, reading, and signing schedule, news of how the book is doing, etc. This may be the perfect time for you to start a newsletter. You have your mailing list of purchasers, clients, friends, and associates—put it to good use with more PR. Your newsletter will keep your name in front of your market audience, as well as showcase some of your abilities. Let your newsletter be a reflection of your personality and convey your enthusiasm for your topic. This is a good place to put endorsements, testimonials, and quotes from reader's letters. If creating a newsletter makes sense for your topic, you need to consider what kind of exclusive information you'll offer readers. Newsletters have a simple, clear, concise writing style. You'll need to create a newsletter design that pulls readers from page to page. And remember, a newsletter's value is in providing news that they want but can't get anywhere else. If another book is in the works, you may start with early promotion to your eager and waiting fans. Be careful, though, to be successful you need to have at least as much newsworthy information as you do your promotional news. Have a catchy title, keep your newsletter small, produce it attractively and regularly, and have it budget-priced if you want to get maximum attention and create a hit.

Before you begin a newsletter ask yourself:

1. Do I really have something to offer and will my ideas fill a void?

2. Who and what is my competition?

3. Do I know how I'll reach my audience?

4. Will a newsletter add a benefit to my book(s) and speaking or will it become a burden and distraction?

5. Do I have the budget to make this work—or will I have to charge too much to use it as an effective publicity tool?

6. Who will my readers be?

7. Am I willing to make a commitment to this and make it more than a one-time effort?

There are a lot of valuable resources to help you in developing your newsletter. Check your public library or bookstore for the wide selection.

Editing Your Newsletter (4th edition), Mark Beach, Writer's Digest Books, 1995, $22.95. How to produce an effective publication using traditional tools and computers. How to produce an effective, professional publication—on schedule and on budget—including: setting your publication's goals, developing reader-appropriate stories, combining text and graphics, creating designs and headlines that grab readers, a new section on story ideas and angles that work.

Marketing With Newsletters (2nd edition), Elaine Floyd, Writer's Digest Books, $29.95 (CAN $42.99). Dynamic methods for boosting sales, building membership, raising donations, and getting the word out with a printed, e-mailed, faxed or Web site newsletter.

Newsletter Editor's Handbook (5th edition), Marvin Arth, Helen Ashmore, and Elaine Floyd, Writer's Digest

Books, $24.95 (CAN $35.99). A quick-start guide to news writing, interviewing, copyright law, volunteers, and desktop design.

Publishing Newsletters ... A Complete Guide to Markets, Editorial Content, Design, Printing, Subscriptions, Management, and much more, Howard Penn Hudson, Charles Scribner's Sons, 1982, $19.95.

Quick and Easy Newsletters, Elaine Floyd, Writer's Digest Books, $34.99 (CAN $51.99). A step-by-step, software-compatible system for creating a newsletter in an afternoon. IBM/Windows compatible disk, 20 templates, 3 cartoons, 30 clip art images, 10 inspirational quotes and 5 filler articles.

Use Business Cards

Some authors are reproducing the cover of their book on one side of their business card. Other writers choose to list book titles they are currently promoting. Be creative and original. No one says business cards have to be just black ink on white stock any more.

Design your business card to be a mini-ad of your book and its features. Give them away lavishly not only as a source of contact information, but also as a great tool for advertising your book. Business cards may be personally handed out at all gatherings, placed on bulletin boards in public places, distributed at places where your potential customers gather, even left with your tip when you leave a restaurant. Your business card should always be in your hand at the first point of contact when you are being introduced to a new acquaintance. At conventions, conferences, and trade shows, exchange business cards with every person you talk to.

Develop Useful Specialty Products

These marketing gimmicks are everywhere and being used by everyone—why not you? Other authors do. Best-selling romance writer Debbie Macomber has given away everything from aprons to lunch bags and bank deposit bags. In a recent press release about a new tea gift book, I received two tea bags. Figure out a clever tie-in with your book title and go for it. It's a source of constant advertising. Anything that has your name on it, tells what you do, and gives some information about your book is an awareness-builder for you. Items that have worked well include: bookmarks, letter openers, ball point pens, calendars, key chain tags, coffee mugs, baseball caps, T-shirts, and computer mouse pads. One Christian bookstore gave women an emery board on which was placed this wording: "Smooth out the rough edges of life at Lighthouse Christian Stores." If you want to spend more to reflect a "high-end" profile, leather date books or leather portfolios are useful constant advertisements.

Your bank account is the only limit. Don't spend too much at one time. This should be only a small part of your total advertising campaign. There are thousands of items to choose from and you can find sales representatives for these products in your telephone book yellow pages under "advertising specialties."

Develop Key Contacts with the Influencers

Often our best source of word-of-mouth advertising comes from people who influence our target audience. This is especially true if you are an unknown and your book is for a specific Christian audience. So take the leaders to lunch—

pastors, youth leaders, worship ministers, lay leaders, Christian counselors, anyone who is a key gatekeeper to the people you want to reach. Don't forget to thank them for their time by giving them an autographed copy of your book. Be sure to develop a quick and easy-to-read brochure that you can leave in their hands, and that they can use for passing the information along to their constituencies. Never forget that none of us had heard of Frank Peretti and *This Present Darkness* (Crossway Books) until he was discovered by Amy Grant and she started talking about his book in all of her concerts—then he became a household name.

Partner with Other Author/Speakers

Authors who are speaking and promoting their books are creating instant excitement and instant awareness. As we've already discussed, a lot of extra income can be derived by sales at the autograph table after a lecture. Many authors who would have only one or two books to sell are finding that mutual promotion of other author/speaker's books can work to their advantage. Consumers are drawn to tables that showcase a lot of colorful, attractive book titles, and where there is lots of variety to choose from. Normally the person doing the selling for you will take them on a consignment basis and you will give them a commission based on the number of sales they generate. Sally Stuart, author of *Christian Writers' Market Guide* (Harold Shaw), has very successfully worked this to her advantage wherever she goes to speak. Her table is filled with not only her own books on the writing business, but also books by dozens of other authors. At the Mount Hermon Christian Writers 2000 Conference, Sally placed twenty-two titles on consignment.

Stay Involved with Events That Make the News

The key to obtaining publicity (a.k.a. free advertising) for your book is to create stories that the media want to cover, according to John Nardini, vice-president of marketing for Chordant Distribution Group in Nashville. Get involved with a charitable organization in helping others, particularly if you can make a significant contribution. What are you doing to serve your community: volunteering at the Chamber of Commerce, helping under-privileged kids, volunteering as a teaching author in the public school? How can you make a tie-in to your book through these events? Sponsor some kind of large event that will attract the media.

Look for the unusual in your story (i.e. 86-year-old publishes first book), or unusual research, or unusual events for your part of the country. Submit stories of attending the CBA International Convention to your local paper. CBA is a BIG event and many people are surprised when they hear that Christian product sales exceed $3 billion annually. Obviously, you'll want to have them mention that you are a local author attending the event. Make sure that you are either making news or finding a news hook that you can piggyback on. News that is about to happen or already happening is a good opportunity for publicity.

ROBERT BOARDMAN

Robert Boardman is able to capitalize on all historical events surrounding World War II when publicizing his book, *Unforgettable Men in Unforgettable Times ... Stories of Honor, Courage, Commitment, and Faith from World War II*. Bob was a Marine who fought in the battles of Cape Gloucester, New Britain; Peleliul, and Okinawa with the First Tank Battalion, First Marine Division. The division received three presidential unit citations. Boardman was personally decorated with the Silver Star and two Purple Hearts. He painstakingly researched, interviewed, and collected stories of Marines who fought with him in that truly unforgettable war against the formidable Japanese enemy. (Available from the author, Robert Boardman, PO Box 25001, Seattle WA 98125-1901; $12.99, plus $3 shipping.)

TEN

It's a Book by Book by Book Sales Process

There are no shortcuts in this business, no easy way out. It will be hard work, but many authors consider getting their book into the hands of their readers the most rewarding thing they will do in this lifetime. You've seen self-published books with an order blank in the back. Order blanks sell books. Some authors find that their in-book order blank brings in more sales than a brochure. Friends tell friends or friends see the book and want a copy for themselves. The order blank makes it easy to get. Customers may now send money instead of writing or e-mailing to ask how they may order the book. The order blank is always on the last page of the book—facing out.

What About Classified Ads?

The main objective of a classified ad is to pull in inquiries about your book. People generally respond, though not in huge numbers, by requesting more information. Your ad should be designed to seek inquiries, not orders. There is not enough room in a small classified ad to give all the details required to secure and service an order. You have a better chance if you state the title and subtitle succinctly, then offer free information to any potential buyers who want more details.

Ads are a definite challenge to write. In a few brief words you must grab, challenge, and move to action. Successful ad writers use a proven formula of: attract attention, generate interest, and stimulate desire, then ask for their action. As with all writing, you have only a few seconds for your headline to grab the reader's attention. In strong headlines, the use of power words will emphasize your benefits. If you write an ad, make it compelling. Then invite response and lead the reader to action.

It is important that you have your brochure or flier ready when your ad is run. All requests for information should be responded to immediately. The classified ad helps you determine your book's sales appeal and potential. The quality of your brochure or flier that you return through the mail will greatly affect your order rate. Most classified ads by self-publishers are run to build a good mailing list of prospective buyers, and not primarily to sell books. Much discussion has been made over whether classified ads pull in different inquiries than a display ad would if ran in the same issue. Never assume that a classified ad under a certain heading in one magazine will automatically pull as well in the same classified heading in another publication. Audience interests differ greatly from one publication to another. Check your competition in the classifieds and make sure that you come up with something more catchy, attractive, and with considerably more benefits. Trace your inquiries and find out what works best for you.

As a one book author, you will probably not be able to afford many (if any) display (or space) ads. These can be very expensive and you can spend a lot of money in a hurry, with very little returns. "Few self-publishers rely on space advertising except in highly specialized media directed specifically to large numbers of their prime target market," says Jerod Rosman, author of three self-published books, including *How to Self Publish Your Book Successfully.*

Self-promotion guru John Kremer, in his valuable book, *1001 Ways to Market Your Books,* says, "All it take is five promotions a day. Really, that's all it takes. Mail a letter. Send out a news release. Phone someone. Take an editor to lunch. Do a phone interview. Give a speech. Jot down a postcard. It need not require much time—15 to 20 minutes is enough—but it can make a world of difference on how well your book sells" (p. 251).

Now That You're a Self-Publishing Entrepreneur—You'll Want to Read at Least Some of These Books

1001 Ways to Market Your Books ... For authors and publishers, John Kremer, Open Horizons, P.O. Box 205, Fairfield, IA 52556. (515) 472-6130; 1-800-796-6130. Fifth edition, 1998, $27.95. www.bookmarket.com. Step-by-step guide on how to do your own marketing.

A Christian Writer's Manual of Style, Bob Hudson and Shelley Townsend, Zondervan, 1988, $16.99, softcover,

208 pp. A standard reference guide for anyone involved in journalism, publishing, and communications in general. These editors systematically present what other style books ignore. How do you handle the capitalization of the deity pronoun? How do you obtain permission to quote from published hymns, poems, or books? Find out fast with this completely indexed guide. www.zondervan.com/academic/350212.htm.

A Simple Guide to Marketing Your Book ... What an author and publisher can do to sell more books, Mark Ortman, Wise Owl Books, Box 29205, Bellingham WA 98228-1205. (360) 671-5858. OWLBOOKS@aol.com, $9.95, plus $4.00 shipping. www.wiseowlbooks.com/publish.

A Simple Guide to Self-Publishing (2nd edition) ... A time and money-saving handbook to printing, distributing and promoting your own book, Mark Ortman, Wise Owl Books, Box 29205, Bellingham WA 98228. (360) 671-5858. $9.95, plus $4.00 shipping.

Business & Legal Forms for Authors & Self-Publishers, Tad Crawford, Allworth Press, New York, 1990, $15.95.

The Chicago Manual of Style ... The essential guide for writers, editors, and publishers (14th edition), University of Chicago Press, 1993.

The Complete Guide to Self-Publishing, Third Edition, 1994, Tom and Marilyn Ross, Writer's Digest Books, $18.99. Includes an excellent "Publishing Timetable" to show you what to do and when.

The Economical Guide to Self-Publishing ... How to produce and market your book on a budget, Linda Foster Radke, Five Star Publications, 4696 West Tyson St., Chandler AZ 85226. 1996, $19.95, plus $3.00 shipping. 1-800-545-7827 or (602) 940-8182.

For All the Write Reasons ... Forty successful authors, publishers, agents, and writers tell you how to get your book published, Patricia C. Gallagher, Young Sparrow Press, PO Box 265, Worcester PA 19490. 1992, $24.95, plus $3.00 shipping. (215) 364-1945.

From Book Idea to Bestseller ... What you absolutely, positively must know to make your book a success, Snell, Baker & Baker, Prima Publishing, 1997, PO Box 1260, Rocklin CA 95677. $18.00. (916) 632-4400.

How to Sell Your Book ... Through Easily Booking Christian Radio Interview Shows, Dr. Millard MacAdam, ProActive Leadership, 1998. Including data base disk, $39.95. Features fifteen short, idea-filled chapters to help authors easily book and conduct radio interviews and sell more books. Plenty of examples and illustrations to guide the entire process. Proven strategies help authors more quickly and easily reach the audiences of over 200 stations. The book includes a "ready-to-go" disk for easily bringing a database of "vitals" for Christian talk shows across America—hosts who want to interview authors. A time-saving "tool kit" for Christian authors. Order from ProActive Leadership, 2114 Vista Laredo, Newport Beach CA 92660-4041. Include $6.00 for postage and handling.

Jump Start Your Book Sales ... A money-making guide for authors, independent publishers, and small presses, Marilyn and Tom Ross, Communication Creativity, PO Box 909, Buena Vista CO 81211. 1-800-331-8355. 1999, $19.95.

Publish to Win ... Smart Strategies to Sell More Books, Jerrold R. Jenkins, Rhodes & Easton, 121 E. Front St., Fourth Floor, Traverse City MI 49684. 1-800-706-4636. $20.00. Proven marketing strategies for writers and publisher who want to discover the newest and most profitable ways of selling their books.

The Self-Publishing Manual ... How to write, print, and sell your own book, Dan Poynter, Para Publishing. Sixth printing, 1991, $19.95. One of the best-known titles of the self-publishing industry—everything you need to successfully write, publish, and sell your own book.

So You Want to Self-Publish ... How to avoid the pitfalls, experience the joys, and make money at self-publishing, Steve Meyer, Meyer Publishing, 304 East Maple, Garrison IA 52229. 1997, $14.95. About this book, Dan Poynter, author of *The Self-Publishing Manual,* says, "Refreshingly direct, exceptionally useful and fun to read. At last a book that tells it like it is by a veteran from the publishing trenches."

The Writer's Legal Guide, Tad Crawford and Tony Lyons, Revised Edition, 1996, Writer's Digest, $19.95.

Writerspeaker.com, Carmen Leal, 2000, Harold Shaw/ WaterBrook Press. A combination of stories and lists offering simple explanations on using search engines, e-mail, mailing lists, forums, Web sites, chat rooms, news groups, and more. Contains a selection of helpful Web sites conveniently categorized. Each chapter features a topical overview, a review of related Web sites, and stories and examples from writers and speakers on how they have used the Internet to attain their publishing and speaking goals.

The Writer's Workbook ... A Full and Friendly Guide to Boosting Your Book's Sales, by Sensible Solutions' Judith Appelbaum and Florence Janovic, 1991, Pushcart Press, PO Box 380, Wainscott NY 11975. Distributed by W.W. Norton & Co., 500 Fifth Avenue, New York NY 10110. For people being published by multinational giants, by small presses, or by themselves.

Periodicals You'll Want to Read

CBA Marketplace: PO Box 200, Colorado Springs CO 80901. (719) 576-7880; FAX: (719) 576-0795; publications@cbaonline.org; www.cbaonline.org. For non-member subscription, send $50.00. Colorado residents add 3% sales tax. International add $30/year surface rate, $60/year airmail. Canadian add $16.50/year. Checks must be drawn on a major U.S. bank.

Christian Retailing: To subscribe, send $75 per year (20 issues) to Christian Retailing, Subscription Service Department, PO Box 420234, Palm Coast FL 32142-0234. Allow four to six weeks for your first subscription copy to be delivered.

NRB (National Religious Broadcasters): Published monthly except March and August. To subscribe, send $24 for one year to NRB, 7839 Ashton Ave., Manassas VA 20109-2883. Canadian orders add $6.00 annually; other international orders add $24.00 per year.

Publishers Weekly: The International News Magazine of Book Publishing and Bookselling. For fast ordering, call toll-free 1-800-278-2991 (Continental U.S. only. All others, call 1-818-487-4557). Or send $189 to Publishers Weekly Subscriptions, PO Box 16178, North Hollywood CA 91615-9672. Canadian subscription rate: $239 for one year (includes GST). All other countries: $319 for one year (includes air delivery). Remit in U.S. funds only.

The WIN-INFORMER: The official communication of Writers Information Network (WIN), the Professional Association for Christian Writers. The *WIN-INFORMER* publishes marketing news, trends, and industry information to aid writers with their publishing and speaking careers. Published four or five times a year by Writers Information Network. Subscription rate: $35 per year, $40 per year in US funds, if mailed to Canada or internationally. Writers Information Network, PO Box 11337, Bainbridge Island WA 98110. E-mail: writersinfonetwork@juno.com; or Web site at: www.bluejaypub.com/WIN.

Publicists You May Want to Contact and/or Hire

Marketing and advertising consultants, also known as publicists, have become the norm even in the CBA industry. Often your publicist will become your best ally in your quest for getting your name out there and establishing the recognition that builds sales. The creative talents that go into the book marketing world are a totally different type of writing creativity than was needed for you to write the book.

There are lots of former publishing house publicists and other marketing specialist now working as freelancers in the publishing industry. Before you settle on the person and type of advertising that is right for you and your book product, shop around. Ask questions. Get references. Check the track record of anyone you are considering hiring to manage your marketing and advertising efforts. Of course, there can be no guaranteed results in public relations efforts, but generally the efforts of your publicist will pay off.

Marketing advice does not come cheap—so you'll want to be sure you'll be happy with what you will have to pay for—results or not! A publicist will basically do the same thing that you could do for yourself. But because of a publicists research, planning, and experience, they can take some shortcuts, get some breaks, and do the job more efficiently and effectively than you would be able to. Many publicists charge between $1,000 and $3,000 for their monthly retainer fee—expenses such as postage, travel, etc. will be added on top of that fee. Most publicists have a stable of clients they're working with all the time, so it could take a month or more for them to read your book, become familiar enough with you and your materials, and then begin writing up all your media kit materials.

But if you need help in: developing interview angles and marketing ideas that can broaden your consumer base; perfecting your interview techniques so that the listeners are drawn in and enticed to purchase your book; focusing publicity efforts in the big radio markets; or designing the type of press material that will grab the busy producer's attention, then you may want to look into hiring the services of a

Media Consultant or Publicity Firm. Always ask what type of publicity campaign they have to offer that will match your needs and your budget. Some well-known publicists in the CBA market include:

Gina Adams, The Adams Group
PO Box 110707
Nashville TN 37222
(615) 331-3314; FAX: (615) 331-9080

Advocate-Media Group
90-8 Ventures Way #9
Chesapeake VA 23320
(888) 863-2988

Patricia Avery, Avery PR
1-800-672-8379 in Colorado Springs, or
averypr@uswest.net

A. Larry Ross & Associates, Inc.
Larry Ross or Christine Moore
4010 Midway Rd.
Carrollton TX 75007
(972) 267-1111; FAX: (972) 267-3535

Ambassador Agency
Jessica Atteberry, Executive Director
Ambassador Public Relations
PO Box 50358
Nashville TN 37205
(615) 370-4700; FAX: (615) 661-4344
Jessica@AmbassadorAgency.com
www.AmbassadorAgency.com

B&B Media Group
1200 Lexington Square
Corsicana TX 75110
1-800-927-0517
FAX: 1-800-8827-3742
Terry Walsh, Midwest Office (608) 236-0950
237 W. Sunset
Madison WI 53705
Louise Ferrebee, Chicago Office (630) 690-0642
E-mail: tbbmedia@airmail.net or tbbmgmag@juno.com

Divisions that specialize in all your communication needs include: Broadcast and Print Publicity, including Media Tours; Radio and Print Advertising Campaigns; Quality Program Production; Strategic Marketing Campaigns. First Edition features one-on-one interviews with notable authors and dramatized productions for fiction titles.

Ruth Ann Bowen, The Bowen Agency
4975 Tanqueray Lane
St. Louis MO 63129
(314) 416-7378; FAX: (314) 416-7375
thebowenag@aol.com

The Bowen Agency specializes in crafting and executing highly customized and personalized public relations plans. They can serve all your media service needs including press releases, securing and organizing interviews, phone follow-up with contacts, and mailings. Handles radio and television media coverage.

Don Otis, Creative Resources Inc.
Consulting and Media Services
PO Box 1665
Sandpoint ID 83864

(208) 263-8055; FAX: (208) 263-9055
CMResource@aol.com

A Christian publicity firm that schedules more than 1,700 broadcast interviews annually and arranges numerous reviews, articles, and interviews in major publications. Also provides services for direct mail, communications, and media relations to parachurch groups, publishers, broadcast ministries, and select corporations.

Fresh Impact Communications
Scott B. Spiewak, President
17 Meadow St.
Harrison NY 10528
(914) 835-4564; FAX: (914) 835-6131
spiewaks@gateway.net

Jacqueline Cromartie, Jakasa Productions
108 Fairview Parkway
Lafayette LA 70508
(318) 981-6179

McClure/Muntsinger Public Relations
Jana Ford Muntsinger
Pamela McClure
PO Box 804
Franklin TN 37065
(615) 370-0043; FAX: (615) 376-9443
jana@mmpublicrelations.com
pamela@mmpublicrelations.com

Judy Waggoner, Premier Marketing Public Relations
2520 Crestview Dr.
Appleton WI 54915-3065

(920) 991-2614; FAX: (920) 991-2615
GrfieldMom@aol.com
Provides marketing advice to the Christian book industry.

JOHN KREMER

John Kremer, author of *1001 Ways to Market Your Books*, in his "Book Marketing Tip of the Week" (February 7, 2000), says: "Don't rely just on publicity. You'll probably need to do some direct mail as well. Also some speaking. Then more publicity. Even after 15 years of persistent marketing, I've still probably reached no more than 50% of all publishers. Unfortunately, there is no magic to selling books. It's lots of work, a modicum of luck, plenty of persistence, and a groundswell of word of mouth. If you are not willing to commit two to three years marketing a book important to you, then you shouldn't publish it."

ELEVEN

Promoting and Selling Your Book in Canada

Contributed by Gus Henne

The Christian Bookstore Industry in Canada

In many ways, the Canadian book market is similar to our neighbor to the South. Christian bookstores are as reluctant to carry individual author's books, and Canadian distributors even more so.

The Canadian Chapter of the Christian Booksellers Association (CBA) records approximately 222 member bookstores and 328 non-member stores.

Christian Booksellers Association
679 Southgate Drive, Guelph ON N1G 4S2

Bookstores prefer to purchase their books from distributors and/or publishers because they would rather deal with fewer suppliers.

The CBA directory lists over twenty-five distributors to the trade. However, less than ten are independent distributors able to even consider individual author's books.

IMPORTANT: When bookstores buy books, they expect a minimum 40 percent discount. Distributors expect anywhere from 10-20 percent on top of that. This means that, unless your book is priced at least three times the printing cost, you will lose money with every sale.

Many authors have found that selling through bookstores is not worth the time and returns. Distributors and bookstores do not pay on delivery for books. They expect to be invoiced and will not pay until the books have been sold—sometimes three to six months after delivery. Also, books can returned by the bookstore—many times in unsalable condition.

Publicity and Book Reviews

You have the best chance of getting a book review in your local newspaper, or in the larger papers that pay attention to the literary arts. Depending on the subject matter, other newspapers may review books that they feel will fit their audiences. A query letter with a SASE will let you know quickly whether it is worth sending them material. For a large list of contact names and addresses, consult: *CARD, Matthew's,* the *Canadian Almanac,* or the *Corpus Almanac.*

Publications which carry pre-publication reviews and are read by booksellers and librarians:

Access
100 Lombard St., #303
Toronto ON M5C 1M3

(416) 363-3388
In British Columbia: 1-800-387-1181
FAX: (416) 941-9581

Books in Canada
603 - 130 Spadina Ave.
Toronto ON M5V 2L4
(416) 601-9880

Canadian Author
1225 Wonderland Rd. N.
PO Box 8029
London ON N6G 4X1
A quarterly magazine with a regular markets feature that updates the current scene in both the magazine and book fields in Canada. Reviews poetry books in its "Canadian Poetry" section and also reviews books about writing and publishing.

Canadian Bookseller
Canadian Booksellers Association
301 Donlands Ave.
Toronto ON M4J 3R8
(416) 467-7883; FAX: (416) 467-7886

Emergency Librarian
810 Broadway W., #284
Vancouver BC V5Z 4C9
FAX: (604) 925-0566

Quill & Quire
70 The Esplanade, 4th Floor
Toronto ON M5E 1R2
(426) 360-0044; FAX: (426) 360-8745

Other Sources of Information

The Book Trade in Canada
Ampersand Communications Inc.
5606 Scobie Cres.
Manotick ON K4M 1B7
An annual updated publication of the publishing industry in Canada (similar to Literary Market Place).

The Canadian Writer's Guide
Fitzhenry & Whiteside
195 Allstate Parkway
Markham ON L3R 4T8
The official handbook of the Canadian Authors Association aimed at helping writers.

The Canadian Writer's Market
McClelland & Stewart
481 University Ave.
Toronto ON M5G 2E9
Lists periodicals and book publishers.

GUS HENNE

Gus Henne has been involved with book publishing for over twenty-five years. His passion is helping writers and authors tell their stories. He is experienced in working with individuals as well as organizations and large corporations, helping them put their books together. For two years, Gus served as the West Coast representative for Essence Publishing. Recently he, along with his wife, Beryl, moved to Ontario where he is Marketing Director for the Essence Communications Group.

Final Word

Books, whether self-published, published by a small press, or a "B" or "C" author published by a major publisher, are most successful when the author gets on the promotion bandwagon and goes full speed ahead with self-promotion. Any writer that becomes well-known in their own corner of the world will be able to move books. But there is not only one method of sales that will make the difference. It is the combination of media events, speaking, and publicity that gets the buzz going and moves book sales. And in today's crowded book marketplace, you'll need to be creative in developing and capturing reader attention.

Index

About the Author

Elaine Wright Colvin is a market specialist, editor, and career consultant for writers/publishers wanting to keep in touch with the changing trends and needs in the Christian writing industry. In 1983, she founded Writers Information Network, The Professional Association for Christian Writers, for which she publishes the *WIN-INFORMER* newsletter. She has directed Writers Conferences and spoken at more than 150 workshops, conventions, Elderhostels, university classes, conferences, and retreats nationwide. She has published hundreds of articles, poems, devotions, and book reviews. She is author, co-author, contributing author, or consultant on more than 35 published books. Her first book was *The Religious Writers Marketplace* (Running Press, 1980). Her most recent, *Treasury of God's Virtues,* August 1998 (now in its third printing), is one of the fastest-selling books of Publications International.

To contact Elaine:

Writers Information Network
PO Box 11337
Bainbridge Island WA 98110
Tel: (206) 842-9103
FAX: (206) 842-0536
E-mail: writersinfonetwork@juno.com
Web site: http://www.bluejaypub.com/win

About Essence Publishing

Essence Publishing is a Christian company dedicated to furthering the work of Christ through the written word. It is our sincere belief that God is the architect of all good things, including technology. Although technology is often used abusively, our responsibility as Christians is to use it for good purposes in obedience to God's call to subdue the earth. Therefore, using modern equipment to its fullest, Essence Publishing believes its mandate is to produce high quality books at very affordable prices.

Much more than just a book printer, Essence Publishing understands the special needs of a successful book. We give specific advice garnered from our experience in publishing and selling books. We look at each book as unique—demanding individual, tailored attention.

Currently, Essence Publishing is one of North America's largest custom book publishing companies. All production is done in house with our own equipment and specialists.

A free *Prospective Author's Guide* is available should you be interested in publishing a book.

You may contact us as follows:

Essence Publishing
44 Moira St. West
Belleville ON K8P 1S3
Toll-free: (800) 238-6376
FAX: (613) 962-3055
info@essencegroup.com
www.essencegroup.com

Order Form

To order additional copies of *A Savvy Approach to Book Sales ... Marketing Advice to Get the Buzz Going*, please use the order form below.

Ordered By: (please print)

Name: _____

Address: _____

City: _____ Prov./State: _____

Postal/Zip Code: _____ Tel.: _____

_____copies @ $12.95Cdn./$9.95US:　　$_____

Shipping ($3.00 first book - $1.00 each add. book):　　$_____

G.S.T. @ 7% (Canadian residents only):　　$_____

Total:　　$_____

Payable by:

❏ Check ❏ Money Order ❏ VISA or ❏ MasterCard

Credit Card #:_____ Exp.:_____

Signature:_____

Send to:　Essence Publishing, 44 Moira St. West
Belleville, Ontario, Canada K8P 1S3

To order by phone, call our toll-free number,
1-800-238-6376
and have your credit card handy.